Releasing the Glory

The Secret of Joy

by Judson Cornwall

Fire Wind™

Mansfield, PA

ISBN: 1-883906-38-5 Releasing the Glory: The Secret of Joy (paperback)
       1-883906-42-3 Releasing the Glory: The Secret of Joy (hardcover)

Fire Wind
P.O. Box 506
Mansfield, PA 16933

(570) 662-7515
(800) 597-1123

http://www.kingdompub.com
email = info@kingdompub.com

Unless otherwise noted, Scripture quotations are from The King James Version of the Bible.

Passages marked NIV are taken from The Holy Bible, New International Version®, Copyright © 1973, 1978, 1984 by the International Bible Society, published by the Zondervan Corporation, Grand Rapids, MI.

Passages marked NKJV are from The Holy Bible, New King James Version, Copyright © 1982, 1985 by Thomas Nelson, Inc., Nashville, TN.

Passages marked Message are from The MESSAGE, The New Testament in Contemporary Language by Eugene H. Peterson, Copyright © 1983 by Navpress Publishing Group, Colorado Springs, CO.

Passages marked TLB are from The Living Bible, Copyright © 1971 by Tyndale House Publishers, Wheaton, IL.

Passages marked Moffatt are from The Bible: A New Translation by James Moffatt, Copyright © 1954 by James A. R. Moffatt. Published by Harper and Row Publishers, Inc.

Passages marked Knox are from The New Testament in the Translation of Monsignor Ronald Knox, Copyright © 1944 by Sheed and Ward, Inc.

Passages marked NRSV are from The New Revised Standard Version of the Bible, Copyright © 1989 by the Division of Christian Education Division of the National Council of the Churches of Christ.

Dedication

I dedicate this book to my son-in-law, Rev. Norbert Senftleben, who envisioned the book out of a brief conversation I had with him. He pressured me out of a self-imposed retirement from writing to produce this book on joy. His encouragement, input, and chapter by chapter editing for content were invaluable. Thank you, Norbert!

Acknowledgments

My special thanks to my wife, Eleanor, for not only releasing me for seemingly endless hours of writing, but for reading each chapter and sharing her comments. I needed to see this truth through the eyes of a woman of God.

Thanks, also, to my secretary, Terri Gargis, who endured repeated editing and rewrites without complaining. You made a valuable contribution to this book.

Table of Contents

Preface

It would take a stretch of the imagination to call America's society joyful. We are pressed by wars and rumors of wars. Shootings fill the daily news reports, and the incidence of killings in our schools make parents more concerned with safety than academics.

We might expect this lack of joy among the godless, but even Christians seem to be living joyless lives. Listening to them talk, we hear of problems, sickness, financial woes, and fears; but seldom do we hear a Christian brother or sister speak of his or her great joy in the Lord. Except for a religious vocabulary, you might think you were talking with a person of the world.

Even our churches seem troubled beyond measure. We hear of dissension, strife, splits, and scandals. Pastors are quitting the ministry in disgust, and thousands of former church members now absent themselves from all church attendance. The shouts of praise and rejoicing of yesterday seem to be replaced with ceremony and complaining.

Are heaven's doors closed to us? Where's the joy that so characterized our walk with Christ after our conversion? Could we be equating happiness with joy and seeking that happiness where the world seeks it? If so, we're doomed to failure, for the world has not found happiness—merely amusement. Happiness is a response to happenings, but the secret of joy involves a response to Jesus.

Joy, true joy, has its origins in God and His Word. Jesus said: *"These things have I spoken unto you, that my joy might remain in you, and that your joy might be full"* (John 15:11). I can find nothing in the Bible that has rescinded this commitment. God's joy is just as available today. Perhaps we have so fixed our gaze on the problems of life that we have forgotten to look unto Jesus, the source and the object of our joy.

Since there is no greater healing power than joy, we need to bring God's joy into the hurts and wounds in our spirits and souls. We also must heed the admonition of the Apostle Paul, *"Finally, my brethren, rejoice in the Lord"* (Philippians 3:1).

Take a relaxing breath and review the Bible's teaching on the source of joy, the characteristics of joy, and the expressions of joy. You'll soon have a life-giving fountain of joy bubbling up in your spirit and spilling over into every area of your life.

Judson Cornwall
Phoenix, Arizona

Introduction

My earlier book, *Ascending to Glory: The Secret of Personal Prayer*, has laid the foundation for this book, *Releasing the Glory: The Secret of Joy*. We redeemed ones are not yet glorious beings, but we have been invited to enter into a measure of God's glory by being in His presence through prayer, praise, and worship. We cannot separate divine glory from the person of God. His glory is but a demonstration of His person and His presence.

Many persons associate God's glory with reactions of fear and dread, but all through five basic divisions of the Bible—historic, poetic, prophetic, gospels, and epistles—persons who experienced a measure of God's glory seem to release that glory through joy.

In the historic books, Moses is the outstanding character to experience the glory of God. On Mount Sinai, he saw God's afterglow. He came down from the mountain so radiant with the light of God that he had to cover his face with a veil. Later in his life, he wrote a Psalm in which he said, *"Satisfy us in the morning with your unfailing love, that we may sing for joy and be glad all our days"* (Psalms 90:14, NIV). The Living Bible translates this, *"Satisfy us in our earliest youth with your loving-kindness, giving us constant joy to the end of our lives"* (Psalms 90:14, TLB, emphasis added). Moses certainly associated experiencing God's glory with releasing that glory in joy.

In the poetic books of the Bible, David speaks much of responding to God in joy. He wrote, *"Thou wilt show me the path of life: in thy presence is fulness of joy; at thy right hand there are pleasures for evermore"* (Psalm 16:11). He also wrote, *"Then will I go unto the altar of God, unto God my exceeding joy: yea, upon the harp will I praise thee, O God my God"* (Psalm 43:4).

He viewed God's presence as the source of his joy, and he recognized that releasing the glory of God's presence could best be served with an expression of joy.

In the Major Prophets, Isaiah was lifted up to God's throne room and saw the Divine glory as few persons have experienced it. He later wrote, *"And the ransomed of the LORD shall return, and come to Zion with songs and everlasting joy upon their heads: they shall obtain joy and gladness, and sorrow and sighing shall flee away"* (Isaiah 35:10). He convinces us that all of God's children will enter into some measure of God's glory, and they will release that glory with greater joy.

The minor prophet Habakkuk spent time with God in his "watchtower" prayer chapel and came out crying, *"Yet I will rejoice in the LORD, I will joy in the God of my salvation"* (Habakkuk 3:18). His circumstances were severe, the vision God had shown him was devastating, but spending time with God in prayer caused this prophet to release the attained glory in unmeasured joy.

In the Gospels, Jesus, who came as a manifestation of God's glory, told His disciples, *"These things have I spoken unto you, that my joy might remain in you, and that your joy might be full"* (John 15:11). The more the disciples realized the glory of God, the greater their joy quotient became.

In the Pauline Epistles, Paul, who had received amazing revelations of God, used the word *Rejoice* more than any other writer in the New Testament. He realized that joy releases the glory that comes from being in God's presence.

The General Epistles also bristle with joy as a release of God's glory. Peter wrote, *"Whom having not seen, ye love; in whom, though now ye see him not, yet believing, ye rejoice with joy unspeakable and full of glory"* (1 Peter 1:8). Even our limited vision of God can be expressed and released in joy beyond our capacity to put into words, but our joyful words will be full of glory.

The only book of prophecy in the New Testament, the book of Revelation, shows the redeemed ones joining the heavenly hosts in singing, waving palm branches, shouting, and praising God. They now live in the divine glory, and their cry is this: *"Let us be glad and rejoice, and give honour to him..."* (Revelation 19:7).

The entire Bible shows that God's glory is not released in power, although, obviously, God is a powerful God. His glory is released through His saints as they joy in Him and express that joy to others. Joy releases God's glory on earth. That is the theme of this book – the source of joy, the characteristics of joy, and expressing that joy.

Section 1

The Source of Joy

1

Joy Is a Noun

"...You removed my sackcloth and clothed me with joy"
(Psalm 30:11, NIV)

The sound of splashing water beckoned me as I walked down the hallway from my hotel room headed for breakfast. Stepping into the large atrium connected to the lobby, I was drawn at once to a large circular fountain with its dancing waters. The sound of splashing water is always relaxing, but the sight of these twelve plumes of water undulating upward from eighteen inches to two feet, with a center fountain that pulsed from eight to twelve feet high, was positively exciting.

Breakfast could wait! My emotions needed to be satiated. Slumping on an upholstered couch, I gazed at the water and let my emotions ride with its rise and fall.

I thought back to the first time I had seen "dancing waters." It was many years ago at the Oregon State Fair, where I was demonstrating Allen organs. I remembered being so entranced with the sight of the waters that I repeatedly went to the display during my break times.

The fountain in front of me in Fort Worth, Texas, was a far simpler installation. Although it was not coordinated to music as at the state fair, still the sight and sound of moving water created ever-changing patterns, playing its own music to my soul.

I began to pray out loud almost involuntarily, "Oh, Lord, let my joy dance before You like these jets of water. May my joy playfully reach up to You like that center plume of water."

The Lord then impressed my spirit with this thought. The water spewing skyward was not joy—it was rather a manifestation of joy: rejoicing. The force that produced this rejoicing was the pump. Without the energy of the pump, the water would remain placid in the pool.

"Lord," I heard myself say, "Now I better understand what the sons of Korah meant when they sang, *'All my fountains are in you'* (Psalm 87:7, NIV). All true joy comes from You. I cannot produce joy any more than this pool of water could, by itself, reach toward the ceiling in such animation."

Defining Joy, a Noun

My friends, we must first realize that joy is an energy, a force, and a power beyond our human ability to generate. When it is present, we are able to release it. What is this thing we call joy? Most Bible dictionaries and encyclopedias begin their definition of *joy* with, "Noun. A positive attitude or pleasant emotion; delight."

One of the by-products of advancing years is the ability to remember events of one's youth. I can vividly recall being seated on the bench of my aged school desk. You've probably seen this old model at one time or another. The top opened like a lid to reveal a storage space underneath and had a two-inch hole drilled at the top right corner to hold the inkwell.

In this memory, I am looking at the back of my teacher who stands at the wall-to-wall blackboard with a fresh piece of white chalk in her hand. In large script letters she writes, "A *noun* refers to a person, place, or thing. A *verb* gives action to that person, place, or thing."

I admit that I have forgotten many things my English teacher taught, but this one phrase sticks in my mind. Nouns and verbs relate together, but they are not interchangeable.

Joy is a noun. *Rejoice* is a verb. Continuing with our dictionary definition, joy is a positive emotion; rejoicing is a release of that emotion—it is activation of that indwelling energy, if you will. We cannot rejoice, though, until we possess joy.

Our King James Bible sometimes seems to use joy as a verb when it speaks of joying in the Lord, et cetera, but the New International Version correctly substitutes the word "rejoice." Actually, the word *joy* is now obsolete as a verb in modern English.

There are so many kinds of joy reported in the Bible that it is difficult to give just a simple definition. Adding to the complexity, varied levels of joy are described, including gladness, contentment, and cheerfulness. Furthermore, joy is always viewed as concrete, not abstract. Sometimes it is spoken of as an individual experience, and at other times, it is seen as a national response. But it never seems to be a mere "attitude." It is rather an attitude jubilantly expressed.

Some years ago, a Christian writer tried to define joy by writing,

Joy is a delight of the mind arising from the consideration of a present, or assured possession of a future good.

When moderate, it is called **gladness**. Raised suddenly to the highest degree, it is **exultation**.

When the desires are limited by our possessions, it is **contentment**; high desires accomplished bring **satisfaction**. Vanquished opposition, we call **triumph**. When joy has so long possessed the mind that it has settled into a temper, we call it **cheerfulness**.

All this is **natural** joy. There is a **moral joy**. This kind of joy is called **peace**; or serenity of conscience. If the action be honorable, and the joy rise high, it may be called *glory*.[1]

This eight-part definition of joy may have come from observation in life or, more likely, the writer may have been aware of the Biblical words used to express this wonderful rise in our emotions. W.E. Vine lists three New Testament Greek nouns for joy and four Greek verbs that we translate as rejoicing, gladness, exultation, joyfulness, and exuberant joy.[2]

Looking in the Old Testament, we find a wealth of Hebrew words for joy. One ancient scholar enumerated ten Hebrew words for joy . . . more realistically, D.W. Harvey lists thirteen Hebrew roots and twenty-seven separate words for joy or joyful.[3]

A great example of the use of these various Hebrew words is seen in Zephaniah 3:14,17 where we find eight different Hebrew words for joy or joyful expression in two verses: *"Sing, O daughter of Zion; shout, O Israel; be glad and rejoice with all the heart, O daughter of Jerusalem. . . The LORD thy God in the midst of thee is mighty; he will save, he will rejoice over thee with joy; he will rest in his love, he will joy over thee with singing."*

Thirteen different Hebrew words for joy in our Bible! Coincidentally, that's the number of jets spraying water into the air in the indoor fountain I so enjoyed. It was all the same water, but it was displayed in thirteen separate plumes, not one of which was exactly like the others. Maybe this can illustrate the differences of joy in our lives.

Joy and Our Emotions

Think of your emotions as the great pool of water from which the fountain bursts forth. It is all the same water, but when that water goes through the pump and out a nozzle, it rises above the pool to varying heights, depending upon the force exerted upon it, and the aperture of the nozzle.

When God moves upon our lives, He draws our emotions into His very nature and then releases them back in expressions of joy. Those expressions will be varied and unique, but they are all mere releases of the joy God has produced by "pumping" us through His nature and back into life. How powerful, beautiful, and even astounding this joyful release is to the observer, especially in this day of tension and anxiety that crushes joy from the life.

Joy is not really optional, and that's good news! We were created with a need for joy. Almost without exception, people want joy. The preamble of our Constitution refers to this as "the pursuit of happiness." In our futile attempt to produce what can be found only in God, we pursue pleasure, possessions, activities, and entertainment. At their very best, these give but momentary delight, but they cannot produce lasting joy. Our emotions must be "pumped" through God to produce a fountain of great joy.

Worship of God is projected in the Bible as touching the deepest springs of emotion, including the feeling of exultant gladness that often finds outward expression in such actions as leaping, shouting, singing, and dancing. Even the Old Testament emphasis upon sacrifice was balanced with great feasting and family celebration. Sorrow for sin was followed by rejoicing in forgiveness. Joy, not judgment, was really the heart of Old Testament worship. Certainly all New Testament worship should at *least* attain this level of exuberance. Jesus came to fulfill all types and symbols of the law—giving us the powerful substance that the law could only project as shadows. Joy is overwhelmingly included in His provision for believers.

The Attitude of Joy

Yes, **joy** is a noun, but it evokes vibrant verbs in expressing itself. The dictionaries may tell us that joy is an attitude; but the Bible speaks of it as an *exuberant* attitude, a very *positive* attitude, an *expressed* attitude. Praise God that it is almost impossible to keep joy hidden! The mouth may keep silent, but the eyes will sparkle.

David, who was a joyful worshiper, reminded us, *"Be glad in the LORD, and rejoice, ye righteous: and shout for joy, all ye that are upright in heart"* (Psalm 32:11). Notice that he did not call for us to shout in order to obtain joy, but to shout because we had joy. When our lives have experienced the great transformation God's redemption brings to us, it is as though the gates of heaven open wide and our emotions spring up like a joyful fountain. Our rejoicing becomes almost involuntary. We feel that we would burst if we did not release it, so great is the inner pressure of joyous delight.

Another psalmist expressed it similarly. *"The LORD hath done great things for us; whereof we are glad"* (Psalm 126:3). It is most likely that this singer was concerned with specific interventions of God into the corporate lives of the Israelites, but perhaps he wrote beyond his full understanding. Yes, we rejoice in God's performance on our behalf. We'll look at that later. This verse suggests to me that our gladness—our joy—is the result of something God is doing deep within us.

"For thou, LORD, hast made me glad" (Psalm 92:4a). God more than releases our joy—He produces it. He takes the dull, drab, and even dismal emotions of our daily life and energizes them with such divine life that they burst forth in exclamations of joy and gladness. God produces joy in joyless circumstances because joy is the result of His redemptive action in us.

Joy needs to be more than an occasional experience for the believer. It should become a lifestyle. We must be more than able to make the *"joyful sound"* (Psalm 89:15)—we need to be *"made . . . joyful"* (Ezra 6:22). Just as the fountain continues to effervesce in what appears to be a continuous flow of water, so God wants our emotions to so continuously flow through Him that joy will become a constant in our lives. Conversely, if we do not surrender our emotions to God, they will become a stagnant pool with all kinds of debris and trash floating on the surface.

God has not redeemed us to become fish ponds filled with lily pads and gold fish. He has equipped us to be overflowing fountains of joy. He didn't save us to become passively serene. His work of grace releases us to be positively joyful.

Far from being slaves of our circumstances; *"...we are more than conquerors through him that loved us"* (Romans 8:37). In Christ, we conquer—even when it appears we are defeated! Wherever we are, whatever we do, we can be joyful in both attitude and expression.

This is a force far greater than happiness. It is also a characteristic present in Christians that is seldom found in the unconverted. Joy does not start in us, nor is it a mere response to happenings around us. It is a force acting upon our lives—changing the way our emotions react and respond to the happenings of life. It is a grand expression of the life of Christ within us and the life to come.

This glorious noun, **joy**, so difficult to describe definitively, always has its beginnings in our God—God the Father, God the Son, and God the Holy Spirit.

For Reflection
1. Can you differentiate between natural joy and moral joy?
2. Who do you see as the most joyful person in the Old Testament?
3. In this chapter I say, "When God moves upon our lives, He draws our emotions into His very nature and then releases them back in expressions of joy." Has this been your experience? When? How?

Endnotes
1. *The People's Bible Encyclopedia*, (1924), emphasis added.
2. *Vine's Expository Dictionary of Biblical Words*, © 1985, Thomas Nelson Publishers, Nashville, TN.

3. *The International Standard Bible Encyclopedia*, Volume 2, pg. 1140, Copyright © 1979 by William B. Eerdmans Publishing Company, Grand Rapids, MI.

2

Joy and God

"Surely you have granted him eternal blessings and made him glad with the joy of your presence" (Psalm 21:6, NIV).

David knew a secret that far too few Christians have yet learned. He excitedly cried, *"Then will I go unto the altar of God, unto God <u>my exceeding joy</u>: yea, upon the harp will I praise thee, O God my God"* (Psalms 43:4, emphasis added). David had learned that God's joy exceeded any pleasure he could find on earth. God is the source of all true joy.

God is a joyful being. I mean it! Think what heaven must be like, for God is filled with joy. You may not sense this in some church services you have attended, but in spite of mournful music and our dire predictions of judgment, God is actually full of joy.

First of all, speaking through His prophets and His Word, God says He is joyful.

"The LORD thy God in the midst of thee is mighty; he will save, he will rejoice over thee with joy; he will rest in his love, he will joy over thee with singing" (Zephaniah 3:17).

Do we need more proof than that? To *"rejoice over thee with joy,"* and to *"joy over thee with singing,"* God must be inherently joyful or He has a source of love unrevealed in the Bible. Since Paul teaches us, *"He is before all things, and by him all things consist"* (Colossians 1:17), we cannot look outside of God for this joy. He is joyful by His very nature.

God assured Isaiah, *"I will rejoice in Jerusalem, and joy in my people"* (Isaiah 65:19).

He also promised Nehemiah, *"The joy of the LORD is your strength"* (Nehemiah 8:10).

If God rejoices over us and shares His joy as a source of strength for our lives, He must, indeed, be a joyful being. For believers, He becomes the source of a heavenly joy.

Additionally, God is joyful in His people. Listen to the psalmists: *"The LORD taketh pleasure in them that fear him, in those that hope in his mercy,"* and, *"The LORD taketh pleasure in his people: he will beautify the meek with salvation"* (Psalms 147:11; 149:4). If your idea of God is that He is a grouch or a judgmental tyrant, you need to replace that concept with a more Biblical one. This is a person so full of joy that He responds very joyfully with His children.

The Joy of His Presence

Our lives become joyful just from being in God's presence. Even though Jeremiah lived in a very difficult period of Jewish history, watching Nebuchadnezzar capture Judah and carry the people to Babylon, there were joyful seasons in his life.

In spite of being misunderstood, imprisoned, and widely mocked, Jeremiah wrote in his memoirs, *"Thy* [God's] *words were found, and I did eat them. Thy word was unto me the joy and rejoicing of mine heart: for I am called by thy name, O LORD God of hosts"* (Jeremiah 15:16). There could be no natural joy in his life at that time, but he had an abundance of divine joy that flowed out of God's Word. He discovered that God and His Word are inseparable.

Believers through the ages have found joy in God. The Old Testament minor prophet said, *"Yet I will rejoice in the LORD, I will joy in the God of my salvation"* (Habakkuk 3:18). The New Testament apostle Paul declared, *"…we also joy in God through our Lord Jesus Christ, by whom we have now received the atonement"* (Romans 5:11). If God is not joyful, how can believers find such joy in their relationship with Him?

Although the Bible does not declare "God is joy" as it declares *"God is love"* (1 John 4:8, 16), there is still much proof that God is a joyful God. His kingdom is said to be a kingdom of joy. (See Romans 14:17.) His heaven overflows with joy. Look in the final book of the Bible and see the choirs singing, the redeemed dancing, and thousands upon thousands of persons waving palm fronds and praising the Lord with a loud voice. If that isn't an indication of joy, I don't know what is!

Furthermore, Jesus affirmed, *"I say unto you, that likewise joy shall be in heaven over one sinner that repenteth, more than over ninety and nine just persons, which need no repentance"* (Luke 15:7). Today, with multiple thousands of persons being daily converted worldwide, heaven is absolutely overflowing with joy. Selah! (Pause and think on *that* for a moment.)

This is not a new concept. God has revealed Himself to be joyful from the beginning of the Bible. There was divine expression of joy when He created the earth. Moses does not record this in the book of Genesis; but Job, who predated Moses by hundreds of years, tells us that when God answered Job out of the whirlwind, He asked where Job had been when God created the earth *"...When the morning stars sang together, and all the sons of God shouted for joy?"* (Job 38:7). In the final book of the Bible, Jesus is called *"the bright and morning star"* (Revelation 22:16*b*). Not only did the angels sing for joy at creation, but also Jesus, the second person of the Trinity, burst into a glorious hymn of rejoicing. What a wonderful picture! It is God's nature to be joyful and, obviously, He also enjoys His work.

Joy Expressed throughout Creation

How can we look at God's creation without being aware of the joy it projects? Picture the babbling brook, the slapping of the ocean waves on the sands of the seashore, and the roar of a cascading waterfall. All are peace producing and joy inducing.

Watch the stallion in the open field prancing and running for the sheer pleasure of it. Witness squirrels playing a fun-filled game of tag in the trees, or observe porpoises or whales swimming playfully in the ocean. Don't you get a feeling that God created them with instinctive joy?

Since we were made in the image of God, we, too, were endowed with joy at the moment of our conception. We can often see this in children at play. No matter whether they are born into poverty or plenty, they have a relaxed, playful spirit—unless an adult represses or suppresses it.

Have you ever met an artist as skillful with the use of color as God? Most mornings my dog, Deacon, and I walk out front to get the morning paper. One day, nudging the paper with his nose, Deacon indicated that something was different. The paper was in a plastic bag. Why? Was the forecast for rain? Looking up, I could barely see scattered, thin, cirrus clouds.

After breakfast, when I walked to my study at the back of our property, I glanced east to see what kind of a sunrise we were having. "Not too spectacular a sunrise today," I thought to myself, for the sun had not yet made its appearance over the horizon. Later, though, taking another look at the sky, I saw the clouds were painted with blushes of pink. It was so beautiful that I brought my wife out to enjoy it with me. The clouds that in the pre-dawn hush had seemed dark, threatening, and ominous had become delightfully beautiful just because the rays of the upcoming sun were highlighting them. "That's what happens when God touches my life," I said to my wife Eleanor.

This is a concept we must grasp. The joy of the Lord does not dissipate the clouds of our lives. It paints them with beautiful hues of God's presence. God shares His very nature of joy with persons who allow Him to shine on and through them.

Joy Versus Happiness

God's joy is not happiness elevated to a high level; happiness is a response to happenings. God's joy is distinctly different. It becomes a display of God's nature in whatever circumstances we may find ourselves. The beauty of joy is not inherent in us; it is reflected upon us. Joy has its beginnings in God Himself, just as the beauty in the clouds that morning was a refraction of sunlight produced by the minute ice crystals in the clouds—giving us the warm, red tones of the rainbow. Is it possible David had this in mind when he wrote, *"weeping may endure for a night, but joy cometh in the morning"* (Psalm 30:5*b*)?

Three times the Psalms speak of being "glad in the Lord." David cried, *"Be glad in the LORD, and rejoice, ye righteous: and shout for joy, all ye that are upright in heart"* (Psalm 32:11), and, *"The righteous shall be glad in the LORD, and shall trust in him; and all the upright in heart shall glory"* (Psalm 64:10). An unnamed psalmist gave as his testimony, *"My meditation of him shall be sweet: I will be glad in the LORD"* (Psalm 104:34). This is not being glad and joyful in what God has done, but just simply glad in the person of God.

Lawrence O. Richards writes: "Joy is an emotion that is evoked by remembering God and his work and by confident expectation that God will act to deliver when troubles come. One's relationship with God, maintained by obedient response to his Word, is a source of joy."[1] Correct relationship with a joyful God will induce joy into our lives.

David learned this source of divine joy, writing, *"My soul shall be satisfied as with marrow and fatness; and my mouth shall praise thee with joyful lips: When I remember thee upon my bed, and meditate on thee in the night watches. Because thou hast been my help, therefore in the shadow of thy wings will I rejoice"* (Psalm 63:5-7).

Remembering God, whether in the daytime or in the night seasons, can be a great source of heavenly joy for us. Television programs and other forms of entertainment may give us a reprieve from pressing circumstances, but meditating on Father God will replace our negative emotions with positive joy. God is the great joy producer. He lights up our lives—not by what He does, but who He is! His joy fulfills our heavenly longings.

The God Who Is Joyous

However, remembering God does not automatically bring us joy, does it? Steve Samson, in his book, *Enjoying God*, observes: "God is misunderstood. Few people understand that God wants us to enjoy Him and He wants to enjoy us. Deceived, we have protected ourselves from getting too intimate with Him, thinking He is going to make life rough on us."[2] I agree:

> This may well have been the attitude of the children of Israel at Mount Sinai when God introduced Himself from heaven and offered them an intimate relationship with Him. Terrorized by the display of the divine Almightiness, they pled with Moses to tell God not to speak to them again. They said that if God would tell Moses what He wanted done, they would do it, for they were professional slaves who were trained to take orders. In this one action, they traded relationship with

God for law from God. They exchanged the joy of relationship for a job based on regulations, and there is little scriptural evidence of joy from then on. Again and again, we read of Israel's murmuring, complaining, and insurrection, but do we hear of them rejoicing with the song and dance after passing through the Red Sea?

Through the pages of church history, those who have embraced religious rules and regulations as their security have displayed little joy. Occasionally, even singing was banned from worship sessions. Religion—with its rites, rituals, ceremonies, and sacred persons—has a way of wringing all joy from the hearts of worshipers, for joy is never the result of performance; it is always the expression of a relationship with God. The more distant that relationship is, the less joy there will be released in worship.[3]

To say that joy is an emotion that is evoked by remembering God, we assume that you have met the loving, gentle, caring God of the Bible, not the exacting, legalistic God of formal religion. In reducing God to a code of rules and ethics, we have often made a harsh dictator or self-righteous judge of Jehovah. We tremble to come before Him because we expect disapproval, judgment, and punishment. Please remember that God is not who you think He is—He is who He says He is!

After spending 40 days on the mountain receiving the Law from God, Moses pleaded with God to see Him. The Lord explained that no man could live through the experience of seeing God directly, so, *"Then the LORD came down in the cloud and stood there with him and proclaimed his name, the LORD. And he passed in front of Moses, proclaiming, 'The LORD, the LORD, the compassionate and gracious God, slow to anger, abounding in love and faithfulness, maintaining love to thousands, and forgiving wickedness, rebellion and sin'"* (Exodus 34:5-7a, NIV).

That doesn't sound like too fearsome a God. He is the One we long to embrace and run to for comfort. Wouldn't you enjoy sitting on His lap, resting your head against His chest? God declares Himself to be filled with compassion, faithfulness, love, and forgiveness. That's the kind of God we can love and enjoy. He is the joy producer, the One who can erase everything that negates joy.

One prerequisite for our living in this joy is to focus on God's self-description and to ignore some of the fearsome, dark pictures being painted by some preachers today. When we see God as He really is, our hearts will overflow with joy! Our Redeemer God is an awesome Being whose nature is brilliant with divine light, glorious in holiness, resplendent in love, and hot with the fire of compassion toward us.

We can find in the Psalms of David many such descriptions of God to enjoy. In a time of great pressure from his enemies, David wrote: *"O send out thy light and thy truth: let them lead me; let them bring me unto thy holy hill, and to thy tabernacles. Then will I go unto the altar of God, unto God my exceeding joy: yea, upon the harp will I praise thee, O God my God"* (Psalm 43:3-4). Rather than flee from God when in trouble, David fled *to* God and found God Himself to be *"my exceeding joy."* So should we. Frankly, we do not need more joy than God can produce in us. One hug from Him can overwhelm us with joy. A word from Him can induce exhilarating ecstasy. Just knowing that He is, indeed, our Father can brighten a dark situation into brilliant hues of divine joy. He is the sunrise; we are the clouds of ice crystals. What a beautiful combination this becomes when we get them together!

It is tragic that religion so consistently misrepresents God, but this is not a new practice. All through the Old Testament, God sought to reveal Himself to the Hebrews, and they consistently misread His nature. They felt that a golden calf was a sufficient representation of the God that brought them out of Egypt. Then, after He gave them the law and ordinances from Mount Sinai, they reduced God to a position of supreme court justice whose task it was to interpret and enforce the law.

When they resisted direct communication, God spoke to them through the prophets, but the people would not listen. After every attempted avenue of self-revelation had failed, God chose to become a person and dwell among us—hoping that through this manifestation, He could reveal Himself to us.

That God-man was Jesus—the second Person of the Godhead. He came to show us God at a level we could understand. Jesus repeatedly told us that the words He spoke were the words He heard His Father speak, and that the deeds He did were simply things He saw the Father do. He told His disciples, *"He that hath seen me hath seen the Father; and how sayest thou then, Show us the Father?"* (John 14:9*b*).

Jesus came as a full representation of Father God, and Jesus was a joyful person.

For Reflection
1. Distinguish between happiness and joy.
2. It has been said that rules without relationship bring rebellion. Do "religious" rules and regulations induce joy or reduce joy in you? What is the difference in David's response in Psalm 119?
3. List three ways you have found God to be joyful.

Endnotes
1. *Zondervan Expository Dictionary of Bible Words*, Copyright © 1985, 1991 by Zondervan Publishing House, Grand Rapids, MI.
2. Steve Samson, *Enjoying God*, Copyright © 1985 by the author and Creation House, Lake Mary, FL.
3. Judson Cornwall, *Worship As David Lived It*, Copyright © 1990 by Judson Cornwall and Destiny Image, Shippensburg, PA.

3

Joy and Jesus

"...that my joy may be in you..." (John 15:11, NIV).

It was a bleak period in Israel's history. The Hebrews were living as a subjugated people under the total domination of Rome, and the control was ruthless. Every attempt to break Rome's power over them ended in a blood bath with thousands of casualties and even more stringent control over their personal lives.

Unheralded and very privately, God, by action of the Holy Spirit, impregnated a young Jewish maiden named Mary. Her baby was born in a borrowed stable in Bethlehem of Judah. Under direction of an angelic visitation, she and Joseph called His name *Jesus.*

Jesus, the Messiah, couldn't have come at a much darker period of Israel's history, and He did not even arrive on a Jewish feast day. Still, the angel of the Lord, resplendent with the glory of God, triumphantly announced to the lowly shepherds on the hillside, *"Fear not: for, behold, I bring you good tidings of great joy, which shall be to all people"* (Luke 2:10).

Many a child's birth has brought joy to the parents and grandparents, but heaven's own messengers sang about the joy Jesus' birth would bring to the whole earth. We could say that Jesus came as a manifestation of God's joy. No wonder, then, that during the Christmas season, we sing Isaac Watts' great carol, *"Joy to the world, the Lord is come!"*

The Jews anticipated that Jesus would overthrow Rome and restore their freedom, but during His entire lifetime, Jesus did nothing to break the rule of Rome. In fact, Jesus did not come to change bad circumstances into happy ones. He came to bring joy, even in the midst of cruelty and tyranny. Jesus proved once and for all that joy and happiness are not synonymous terms. Nothing can crush true joy, and it does not require happy circumstances to stay active. Joy—divine joy—survives anything!

Was Jesus Joyful?

Some years ago, I received a copy of a widely circulated paper, alleging to be an eye-witness account of Jesus, that depicted Him as being serious, sorrowful, unsmiling, and quite disconnected from the real world. The writer quoted Isaiah's description of Christ, *"He is despised and rejected of men; a man of sorrows, and acquainted with grief: and we hid as it were our faces from him; he was despised, and we esteemed him not"* (Isaiah 53:3). This may be an accurate description of Jesus after the whipping post, the crown of thorns, the beard plucking, and the weight of the sin of the world within His being, but it can't describe the life Jesus lived while here on the earth.

I don't know who composed this article, but the author was obviously not a reader of the New Testament. The Gospels show Jesus as a people person loved by men, women, and children. He attended weddings and feasts, but also enjoyed the solitude of the seaside. He had a short life, but I believe He enjoyed it to the fullest.

Can't you see Jesus' eyes sparkle with joy as He watched the lame man take up his bed and walk? Jesus had to get a kick out of seeing a paralytic lowered through the torn up roof by four friends. When children tried to break through the disciples to get a chance to sit on Jesus' lap, His joy must have soared to new heights.

Of course Jesus knew sorrow, but He lived in joy. His joy was not based on position, possessions, or power. Nor was it controlled by circumstances. The source of His joy was His relationship to His Father in heaven and His submission to His Father's will. This intimate union kept Him joyful at all times, no matter what people did to Him. Our ability to live joyfully also depends upon our obedience to Father God and our love for Him.

Joy was actually a motivating force in the life of Jesus. We read, *"Looking unto Jesus the author and finisher of our faith; who for the joy that was set before him endured the cross, despising the shame, and is set down at the right hand of the throne of God"* (Hebrews 12:2).

It may be correct to see this verse holding joy before Jesus as a future reward that induced Him to endure all the ignominy of His mission here on earth, but isn't that pretty much a carrot-on-a-stick syndrome? It is far more likely that Jesus was the possessor of glorious divine joy, and He chose to keep that joy paramount in His consciousness. The further He proceeded into the known will of God, the more intense and glorious that joy became.

We are comfortable in depicting a person's mood by his speech and the stories the person tells. Put this test to Jesus. He spoke lovingly about His heavenly Father. He loved to use the word "*blessed*" when talking to persons. He was an encourager to the discouraged, a comforter to the distressed, and a source of healing to the sick. His speech could be severe to the hypocrites, but it was a soothing balm to the sinners. His speech was joyful.

And His stories? They were about celebrations. He told about the woman who found her lost coin, the shepherd who located his stray sheep, and the merchant who found the pearl of great price. They were stories with a joyful ending.

His parables were equally joyful and full of celebration. He told of the great wedding feast where persons were pressed to come in and join the festive celebration. He told of the prodigal son being received back home with an enormous celebration, indicated by the robe, ring, and the festive slaughter of the fatted calf. These kinds of stories come out of the heart of a joyful person, and Jesus, the storyteller, was immensely joyful. His stories, of course, illustrated great spiritual truths—joyful truths.

Our Inheritance of Joy

In the final talk Jesus had with His disciples before His arrest and crucifixion, He told them, *"These things have I spoken unto you, that my joy might remain in you, and that your joy might be full"* (John 15:11). Jesus could not have imparted a joy He did not possess. He offered them and us a union with God similar to the one He enjoyed. He was offering His disciples a double joy—His joy and their joy full to the brim.

Commenting on this passage, Oswald Chambers said,

What was the joy that Jesus had? It is an insult to use the word happiness in connection with Jesus Christ. The joy of Jesus was the absolute self-surrender and self-sacrifice of Himself to His Father, the joy of doing that which the Father sent Him to do. *"I delight to do Thy will."* Jesus prayed that our joy might go on fulfilling itself until it was the same joy as His. Have I allowed Jesus Christ to introduce His joy to me?[1]

This joy is now obtainable. In His High Priestly prayer to the Father, Jesus said, *"And now come I to thee; and these things I speak in the world, that they might have my joy fulfilled in themselves"* (John 17:13). Can you think of any prayer that Jesus prayed that the Father did not answer? Jesus demonstrated the joy of intimate, personal union with the Father and then prayed for it to be available to us. We can live in His joy at all times.

This is a priceless gift, but we not only have Christ's demonstrated and imparted joy, we have the joy of His person. Peter, who spent years with Jesus as a disciple, wrote in his old age to believers who never had the privilege of seeing Jesus: *"Whom having not seen, ye love; in whom, though now ye see him not, yet believing, ye rejoice with joy unspeakable and full of glory"* (1 Peter 1:8).

I well remember the days of my youth when the congregations in the churches my father pastored used to sing these words of Peter with great gusto. Those congregations seemed to be aware of the joy of the Lord, and delighted in expressing it in many songs of joy. Merely believing in Jesus induces *"joy unspeakable and full of glory."* Can this be said of any other person in history?

This joy, made available to believers, is based on a relationship with the triune God.

Oswald Chambers reminds us that Paul wrote: *"Christ Jesus . . . is made unto us wisdom, and righteousness, and sanctification, and redemption"* (1 Corinthians 1:30). Then Chambers says, "When we realize that Christ is made all this to us, the boundless joy of God begins; wherever the joy of God is not present, the death sentence is at work."[2]

The very person of Jesus is a joy producer. The psalmist knew this, for he wrote, *"Let all those that seek thee rejoice and be glad in thee: let such as love thy salvation say continually, The LORD be magnified"*

(Psalm 40:16, emphasis mine). We do not find the key to real joy in the world or in ourselves. Our joy comes from a much higher source—Christ Jesus Himself.

When fighting depression, sorrow, or gloom, take a long look backward. Remember what you were before Christ came into your life, and then compare it to what has happened to you since He became your Lord. Rejoice in your salvation. You may be temporarily short of happiness, but you need never be short of joy.

Jesus, a Fountain of Life

I have already compared our joy to a fountain. It is interesting that in both type and substance, Jesus is spoken of as a fountain. In reviewing the history of Israel's wandering in the wilderness, the psalmist said that God: *"... turned the rock into a standing water, the flint into a fountain of waters"* (Psalm 114:8). When Paul wrote about this incident, he declared, *"...and that Rock was Christ"* (1 Corinthians 10:4). Israel's thirst was quenched by drinking from this supernatural provision of water—a fountain in the desert, and, spiritually, that fountain is Christ.

When talking about God's excellent provision for His people, David wrote, *"... You give them drink from your river of delights. For with you is the fountain of life"* (Psalm 36:8-9, *NIV*). Out of spiritual experience, David realized that God's joy flows in His fountain, and that fountain is Jesus in us—springing up like dancing waters. The emotions of joy are ours, but the energy that makes them a joyful fountain is God's. When we come to Him, He can take our emotions, whether they are positive or negative at the time, and explode them heavenward in rising crests of joy— *"For with you is the fountain of life."* Wouldn't this indicate that without God there would be no life-giving fountain flowing in our lives? We may experience the rise and fall of the emotion of happiness, but God alone is the source of true joy. It rises, refreshes, and then rises anew.

This fountain of joy will flow through eternity. Toward the end of his visions of and in heaven, John heard Jesus say, *"It is done. I am Alpha and Omega, the beginning and the end. I will give unto him that is athirst of the fountain of the water of life freely"* (Revelation 21:6). Pain and sorrow will not follow us into eternity, but joy will, for the fountain of joy is in God the Father, God the Son, and God the Holy Spirit. Eternity is the home of this great triune God. No matter what level of joy we learn to flow in here on earth, it will be like a backyard fountain beside Niagara Falls when compared to the joys of heaven. The best is yet to come!

The joys in Jesus are so abundant that they cannot be fully appreciated here on earth; however, as we turn over more of our lives to Jesus, the fountain of His joys will be greater in us. The greater our submission to His will and way, the higher our fountain of joy will reach upward.

We dare not let sin, self, and pride clog the flow of our emotions into God, for that will disrupt the fountain as surely as if the pump was turned off. Anger, resentment, and an unforgiving attitude will also clog the flow of our emotions into God. We need a clean pool of spiritual emotions— a life that is regularly cleansed by confession and forgiveness—if we want a beautiful fountain of joy surging in our daily experiences of life.

Joy for the believer has its source in God, was demonstrated and applied by Jesus, and is lived out in us by the Holy Spirit. Take the Godhead out of joy and we are reduced to happiness and pleasure. Rather than take the Godhead out of our lives, God sent His Holy Spirit to live in our lives as the actuator of our joys.

For Reflection
1. Jesus offered us double joy. How does that joy come? (See John 15:11)
2. What determines the level of joy we can experience?
3. In this chapter I say, "Jesus was filled with joy to the core of His life." How? Where? When? Could we also be filled with such divine joy?
4. Is there any negative emotion you are holding onto? Any hard feelings toward someone else? Any unforgiveness? Why not surrender these to God? You'll soon experience His divine joy flowing through you.

Endnotes

1. Oswald Chambers, *My Utmost for His Highest*, pg. 178, Copyright © 1935 by Dodd, Mead & Co., Inc., Copyright renewed © 1963 by Oswald Chambers, Publications Association, Ltd.
2. Ibid., pg. 255

4

Joy and the Holy Spirit

"Shout for joy, O heavens; rejoice, O earth; burst into song, O mountains! For the Lord comforts his people…" (Isaiah 49:13, NIV).

I have met few persons who have a problem about God the Father or God the Son, but when we mention God the Holy Spirit, we can get very polarized responses. Some persons rejoice with praise, while others recoil with anger. Perhaps some persons view the Holy Spirit as a function, unction, or anointing, thereby confusing His work with His person. Others have seen extreme physical demonstrations that were blamed on the Holy Spirit. Such displays disgusted them and so they rejected the Holy Spirit.

Still, like it or not, the indwelling of the Holy Spirit is the mark of a New Testament Christian. (For a further description of the indwelling of the Holy Spirit, read Romans 8.) It is not what a person professes that makes him or her a Christian. It is what he or she possesses that makes the difference. Conversion without the indwelling of the Holy Spirit is impossible, for regeneration by the Holy Spirit involves a union with God and Christ that the Bible calls an <u>indwelling</u>. This very union produces immeasurable joy.

We Trinitarians need to be extremely careful lest we inadvertently end up with three gods. The Bible teaches us, *"Hear, O Israel: The LORD our God, the LORD is one"* (Deuteronomy 6:4, NIV), and yet God has revealed Himself as the Father, the Son, and the Holy Spirit. This is, admittedly, a mystery. I find nothing in this life that adequately illustrates it. We must accept it as true because the Bible says it is so.

In my book, *Back to Basics*, I wrote:

The Bible teaches us that the Holy Spirit is one of the three persons of the Godhead. He is divine in the absolute sense, for He has divine attributes ascribed to Him. The Bible calls Him eternal (Hebrews 9:14), omnipresent (Psalm 139:7-10), omnipotent (Luke 1:35), and omniscient (1 Corinthians 2:10-11). God's Word also ascribes divine works to Him. It also credits Him with a part in creation (Genesis 1:2; Job 33:4), regeneration (John 3:5-8), and resurrection (Romans 8:11).[1]

The Mystery of the Trinity: The Persons

The Holy Spirit is a personality separate and distinct from God. He proceeds from God, is sent from God, and is God's gift to persons. Yet the Spirit is not independent of God. He always represents the one God. Just how the Holy Spirit can be one with God and yet distinct from God is part of the mystery of the Trinity.

Pope John XXIII (1881-1963) said, "The Trinity attributes to the Father those works of the Divinity in which power excels, to the Son those in which wisdom excels, and those in which love excels to the Holy Ghost."[2] Martin Luther (1483-1546) wasn't too different in his comprehension of the Trinity. He said, "The Creed confesses three persons as comprehended in one divine essence, each one, however, retaining his distinct personality...to the Father we ascribe the work of creation; to the Son the work of redemption; to the Holy Spirit the power to forgive sins, to gladden, to strengthen, to transport from death to life eternal."[3] It is the Holy Spirit who gladdens our lives. He is also the joy producer.

According to Scripture, the Holy Spirit's specific responsibility is to be *to* and *in* us what He was *to* and *in* Jesus. We normally think of this as empowering and enabling, but the primary work of the Spirit in Christ was to maintain the glorious connection between the Father and the Son. It was this spiritual vitality that kept Jesus joyful under stress, and it will be this intimacy with the Father and the Son that will keep us joyful in this joyless world we live in.

The Holy Spirit is the person in the Godhead charged with living in believers. Jesus told His disciples, and subsequently us, *"I will ask the Father, and he will give you another Counselor to be with you forever—the Spirit of truth. The world cannot accept him, because it neither sees him nor knows him. But you know him, for he lives with you and will be in you"* (John 14:16-17, NIV). Jesus departed so that the Holy Spirit could be imparted. The Holy Spirit is now in believers, serving in the same capacity of helper that Jesus was to His disciples. Imagine that! He teaches us, giving us clearer understanding of the character of God, revealing how we should live, and opening the written Word to us. How desperately we need His presence and intervention in our lives. We'll never live in divine joy without Him dwelling in us.

Without the indwelling Spirit of God, most of us would be unaware that there is a loving, tender God available to our individual lives. Furthermore, we would be far less able to sense or feel the joy of God within us.

Jesus taught us that the believer's heart is the Holy Spirit's home. *"He who believes in Me, as the Scripture has said, out of his heart will flow rivers of living water.' But this He spoke concerning the Spirit, whom those believing in Him would receive..."* (John 7:38,39a). It is this precious Holy Spirit that keeps us from being totally earthbound. Further, unless we have *within* us that which is *above* us, we soon shall yield to the pressures *around* us. Mature believers will testify that when we have the Holy Spirit on the inside, we can stand any kind of battle on the outside.

On the day of Pentecost, Peter declared that after Jesus ascended to the Father, He *"... received from the Father the promised Holy Spirit and has poured out what you now see and hear"* (Acts 2:33, NIV). Promise fulfilled! Power released! Joy unspeakable received!

What is so often overlooked in the coming of the Holy Spirit is that He not only works through us, He also works in us—and He does this very positively. It is His peculiar mission to effect the character and nature of God in our lives. How grateful we are for that mission!

The Fruit of the Spirit

Paul speaks often of this inner change in believers that the Holy Spirit produces, but his metaphor of bearing the fruit of the Spirit gives the clearest picture. In his letter to the church at Galatia, he wrote, *"But the fruit of the Spirit is love, joy, peace, longsuffering, gentleness, goodness, faith, meekness, temperance: against such there is no law"* (Galatians 5:22-23). This is one fruit with nine different manifestations, just as a cluster of grapes has many separate grapes on the stem.

It is easy to see this fruit as three triads. Within the believer, the first three "grapes" to be seen actually ripen toward God—*"love, joy, peace."* The second three ripen toward the person's peers—*"longsuffering, gentleness, and goodness."* The final three ripen toward us—*"faith, meekness, temperance."*

It is a common mistake to refer to these character manifestations as the fruit of a Christian—as though a believer could produce any of these. Quite frankly, none of these are inherent in believers—even "good" believers. This is the *"fruit of the Spirit"* that the Holy Spirit brings into our lives. The first three seem to arrive fully developed, but the rest of them take time to develop and mature.

All fruit is the natural outgrowth of the abiding presence of the Holy Spirit within the life of the believer. Its abundance or scarcity will depend upon our yieldedness to the working of the Holy Spirit in our lives. It is His fruit, not ours, but He is both willing and anxious to transplant it into our being and behavior. It is impossible to bear this heavenly fruit without the abiding presence of the Holy Spirit of God.

Those who know anything about growing grapes know that grapes are propagated by grafting, not by seed. The purpose of bearing grapes, then, is not self-propagation, but for food and for the pleasure of others. Each branch must be grafted into Christ, Who said, *"I am the vine, ye are the branches"* (John 15:5); but the fruit that results out of this uniting is a potential blessing to others. The fruit of the Spirit is produced in the lives of believers to give others a chance to *"Taste and see that the Lord is good"* (Psalm 34:8). How are others to know of the goodness of Christ if they cannot sample some of it in their relationships with believers? [4]

Rather than view the fruit of the Spirit as a transplanted ministry, we should see it as a divine infusion of the very nature of God. God cannot now impart His essential nature to us—His omnipotence, omniscience, omnipresence, et cetera—but He can, and does, share some of His moral nature with believers in whom the Holy Spirit dwells.

Some teachers have said that joy is love *rejoicing* and that peace is love *resting*. This is descriptive of the inter-relational functioning of these forces, but individually and unitedly, they are evidences of the moral essence of the triune God.

True Joy and the Moral Nature of God

The most fundamental characteristic of God's moral nature is His holiness, but intricately associated with and flowing out of that holiness, is God's lavish love, jubilant joy, and perfect peace. We see this in the descriptions of members of the Godhead. The New Testament declares, *"God is love"* (1 John 4:8). The Old Testament gives Jesus the title of *"Prince of Peace"* (Isaiah 9:6), and in the epistles we learn of *"joy in the Holy Spirit"* (Romans 14:17).

When I accept that true joy is part of the fabric of God's moral nature, it becomes evident that I cannot produce joy on my own, just as I am unable to have true love or peace apart from God. If these qualities could be self-produced, I could produce God. Life offers us caricatures of these virtues, but they are artificial, incomplete, and extremely transient. Joy can no more be attained without God than sunshine can be had without the sun. Joy is heavenly born, its aroma is of heaven, it leads to heaven—opening wide its portals—and its emblem is heavenly. How dare we try to manufacture joy on earth? At best, it would be a shoddy counterfeit.

In any event, why should we try to manufacture our own joy when it is available in unlimited abundance from God through the Holy Spirit? God delights in sharing His joyful moral nature with us. He did that at the creation of Adam when, *"The LORD God formed the man from the dust of the ground and breathed into his nostrils the breath of life, and the man became a living being"* (Genesis 2:7, NIV). Adam was alive with the very life of God and God's life is joyful.

Through the work of Calvary and the regeneration of the Holy Spirit, believers are returned to this indwelling life of God. Paul put it so simply when he stated, *"...the Spirit of God lives in you..."* (Romans 8:9, NIV). The breath of divine life that God breathed into Adam, He breathes into each regenerated person. We have the same source of divine joy abiding in us that Adam enjoyed when walking with God in the Garden of Eden. <u>Adam's joy flowed by having fellowship with the voice of God; ours flows from the abiding presence of the Holy Spirit.</u> Although Adam had to wait for God's initiative to come to the Garden, we can initiate our fellowship with the indwelling Spirit at any time.

How marvelous it is for God to share some of His moral nature with us through the fruit of the Holy Spirit. All of the Spirit's fruit is available to any believer in whom the Spirit dwells. If we can become participants in the love of God, we can also participate in the joy of God. If the peace of God has finally dominated our lives, the joy of God can also dominate our emotions.

There is no reason for us to settle for a trade-off where we assign love to one believer, joy to another, and peace to still a third. This triad of fruit comes as a matched set. Where one comes, the others follow. We have been transformed by God's love, and we've been indued with it. Similarly, at conversion we were overwhelmed with divine joy. This same action of God's grace wants to impart that joy as a lasting quality through time into eternity.

What we don't know about God's moral nature, including divine joy, has been taught to us in the Bible. Amazingly, the Bible itself feeds the fountain of joy that bubbles in our inner spirit. The person who lacks an abundant flow of divine joy need only spend time reading the pages of God's divine Book. Joy leaps off the pages of the Bible.

For Reflection
1. What is the second fruit the Holy Spirit brings into the life of a believer?
2. Is the fruit of the Spirit a transplanted ministry, or a divine infusion of the very nature of God?
3. Recount at least three occasions when joy bubbled in your heart while outer circumstances should have made you sorrowful. How do you explain this?

Endnotes

1. Judson Cornwall, *Back to Basics*, p. 64, Copyright © 1994 Sharon Publications and Judson Cornwall.
2. Entries 11426-11428, *Draper's Book of Quotations for the Christian World*, Edythe Draper, Copyright © 1992 by Tyndale House Publishers, Inc., Wheaten, IL.
3. Ibid.
4. Judson Cornwall, *Back to Basics*, p. 64, Copyright © 1994 Sharon Publications and Judson Cornwall.

5

Joy and the Bible

"Your statutes are my heritage forever; they are the joy of my heart"
(Psalm 119:111, NIV).

If our emotions make up the water in the pool and the triune God is the energizing force (the pump) that cascades the water into the air as a beautiful fountain, I suggest that the Bible is the plumbing that gets that water to and from the pump. The Word gets us to God and God to us. God and His Word go together. They are inseparable.

J.I. Packer reminds us, "God the Father is the giver of Holy Scripture; God the Son is the theme of Holy Scripture; and God the Spirit is the author, authenticator, and interpreter of Holy Scripture."[1] God wrote a book to reveal Himself to us, for aside from the Bible, we have no written revelation of God. The Bible is both a true source of joy, and it is a revelation of the God of joy.

Earlier in this book, we looked at the testimony of Jeremiah: *"Thy words were found, and I did eat them; and thy word was unto me the joy and rejoicing of mine heart: for I am called by thy name, O LORD God of hosts"* (Jeremiah 15:16). He certainly was not the first person in the Bible to rejoice at hearing God speak to him or her, but Jeremiah speaks of the written Word of God as being his source of joy and rejoicing. As he ate and assimilated what he read, the very words of the book mysteriously instilled joy in this prophet.

This has also been the testimony of thousands of believers who have learned to see beyond the literal meaning of the words in the Bible—to find a revelation of God and His magnificent provision for His children. When the Bible begins to reveal to us a deliverance from sin and a provision for life as a son of God, the fountain of joy begins to spring up in our spirit.

These divine provisions were ordained by God before the foundation of the world was laid, but they do not become effective in our lives until we know about them. That is why Paul asserts, *"So then faith cometh by hearing, and hearing by the word of God"* (Romans 10:17). Joy explodes in us when we discover in God's Book what a rich inheritance has been left to us through Jesus' sacrifice. We could liken this joy to that of persons who rejoice upon finding that a relative, whom they didn't even know, has left them a small fortune.

Little wonder, then, that the apostle rejoiced, *"O the depth of the riches both of the wisdom and knowledge of God! how unsearchable are his judgments, and his ways past finding out!"* (Romans 11:33). The more we learn of His wisdom, the greater our joy.

"He Spoke a Book"

Not only is the Bible a revelation of the God of joy, it is communication from this God of joy. Repeatedly, the Bible is called "Thy Word," and it is accepted as the final authority— *"For ever, O LORD, thy word is settled in heaven"* (Psalm 119:89). Only God could have inspired the writing of 66 books through about 40 different authors spanning several thousand years and yet maintain one consistent theme—redemption. This great book of His has now been translated into over 1900 languages, and 97% of the world's population now have a sizeable portion of the Bible available in their own language or dialect. What divine provision and joy this has brought to millions of persons!

God not only wrote the Bible, but the Bible is the only book whose Author is always present when it is read. A.W. Tozer declared, "God did not write a book and send it by messenger to be read at a distance by unaided minds. He spoke a book and lives in his spoken words, constantly speaking his words and causing the power of them to persist across the years."[2]

William Law (1686-1761) wrote: "Without the present illumination of the Holy Spirit, the Word of God must remain a dead letter to every man, no matter how intelligent or well-educated he may be... [it] is just as essential for the Holy Spirit to reveal the truth of Scripture to the reader today as it was necessary for him to inspire the writers in their day."[3]

God and the Bible are inseparable. Any attempt to handle them independently will lead to error. Martyn Lloyd-Jones declared, "Nothing is more dangerous than to put a wedge between the Word and the Spirit, to emphasize either one at the expense of the other. It is the Spirit *and* the Word, the Spirit *upon* the Word, and the Spirit in us as we read the Word."[4]

As Don Lyon said, "If you have the Spirit without the Word, you blow up. If you have the Word without the Spirit, you dry up. If you have both the Word and the Spirit you grow up."[5]

This is why I wanted us to look at the part the Bible plays in our joy directly after looking at the Spirit's input to our rejoicing. The Spirit and the Word unite to bring God's heavenly joy into our often lackluster existence. The Bible is a letter from God with our personal address on it. Just seeing the envelope should produce a joyful reaction in us. Lady Jane Grey (1537-1554) said, "The highest earthly enjoyments are but a shadow of the joy I find in reading God's Word."[6]

John wrote: *"These things write we unto you, that your joy may be full"* (1 John 1:4). Paul told the Thessalonian Christians, *"Ye became followers of us, and of the Lord, having received the word in much affliction, with joy of the Holy Ghost"* (1 Thessalonians 1:6). In both cases, the written Word of God and the joy of the Holy Spirit seem to be interconnected. In His parable of the sower, Jesus said, *"But he that received the seed into stony places, the same is he that heareth the word, and anon with joy receiveth it"* (Matthew 13:20). The seed of God's Word is consistently a joy producer.

An unknown author gave us a very succinct overview of the Bible when he wrote:

> The Bible contains the mind of God. The state of man. The way of salvation. The doom of sinners. The happiness of believers. Light to direct you. Food to support you. Comfort to cheer you.
>
> It is the traveler's map. The pilgrim's staff. The pilot's compass. The soldier's sword. The Christian's charter. A mine of wealth. A paradise of glory. A river of pleasure.
>
> Its doctrines are holy. Its precepts are binding. Its histories

are true. Its decisions are immutable. Christ is its grand subject. Our good its design. The glory of God its end.

Read it to be wise. Believe it to be safe. Practice it to be holy. Read it slowly, frequently, prayerfully.

It should fill the memory. Rule the heart. Guide the feet. It is given you in life, will be opened at the judgment, and be remembered forever. It involves the highest responsibility, will reward the greatest labor, and condemn all who trifle with its sacred contents. It is *"the Word of our God which shall stand forever."* [7]

Can we read this description of the Bible without feeling a sense of joy and thanksgiving? Of course not! The whole Bible is a joyous book. Those who see only the dark side of the Bible—judgment, warnings, wars, captivity of nations, et cetera—have forgotten that for an artist to have brilliance in his paintings, he or she starts with a dark background. The picture needs the contrast. Similarly, life is filled with contrasts. We all have dark seasons in our lives, but that does not extinguish the joy—it becomes a backdrop for it. When talking to the disciples about His impending arrest, trial, and crucifixion, Jesus told them: *"These things have I spoken unto you, that my joy might remain in you, and that your joy might be full"* (John 15:11). They were facing a dark season, but there would be exceeding joy at the other end. Jesus wanted them to focus on the coming joy rather than the impending sorrow.

The Bible is a joyful book filled with joyful promises to specific persons and to all believers. Think about the hope, comfort, provision, and eternal rewards guaranteed by God Himself. Don't they produce joy in your life? God's simple promise, *"Never will I leave you; never will I forsake you"* (Hebrews 13:5*b*, NIV), has kept joy in human hearts when circumstances were extremely threatening. Similarly, Christ's guarantee, *"I am going there to prepare a place for you. And if I go and prepare a place for you, I will come back and take you to be with me that you also may be where I am"* (John 14:2*b*-3, NIV), has replaced the pain of dying for many persons with the joy of taking a desired trip.

A Record of Joyful Intervention

This Bible, far more than other literature, records joyful stories. Just look at the book of Exodus and imagine the emotions of the Hebrews the night they were finally released from Egypt. They stepped out of slavery into their first experience with freedom, and they had the wealth of Egypt in their hands. Their flight was with singing, shouting, and flowing tears of tremendous joy. It must have been hard for them to believe that they were finally free and headed to a land of great promise. At the Red Sea, Moses wrote and led the men in singing a song of rejoicing. Miriam, his sister, led the women in playing tambourines and dancing before the Lord (see Exodus 15). It was a time of utter jubilation. So should our salvation be.

Many generations later, God again sent His people into captivity because they had consistently departed from true worship of Jehovah by substituting worship of idols, which were actually representations of demons. This time, after many warnings through the prophets, God sent His rebellious children to Babylon. There they spent 40 years in captivity. Finally, God moved upon the heart of the heathen king to grant these Hebrews permission to return to their own land and rebuild the temple. The returning patriots overflowed with joy. At the groundbreaking ceremony for the rebuilding of the Temple, *"With praise and thanksgiving they sang to the LORD: 'He is good; his love to Israel endures forever.' And all the people gave a great shout of praise to the LORD, because the foundation of the house of the LORD was laid"* (Ezra 3:11, NIV).

So great was this restoration to their homeland that it was made into a song that Jewish pilgrims sang as they came to Jerusalem for one of the three compulsory feasts:

"When the LORD brought back the captives to Zion, we were like men who dreamed. Our mouths were filled with laughter, our tongues with songs of joy. Then it was said among the nations, 'The LORD has done great things for them.' The LORD has done great things for us, and we are filled with joy. Restore our fortunes, O LORD, like streams in the Negev. Those who sow in tears will reap with songs of joy. He who goes out weeping, carrying seed to sow, will return with songs of joy, carrying sheaves with him" (Psalm 126, NIV).

Shouldn't our lives also be joyful after being delivered from the slavery of sin with its compelling habits? When we think each day about how great a salvation we have been given, it would seem that only a conscious repressing of our true emotions could prevent songs, shouts, and joyful behavior that at times seems childish and silly. After all, when joy is released it is not too concerned with formal behavior. (Conversely, the imposition of so-called conventional behavior can often stifle the emotion of joy.)

His Transformational Word

This glorious, miraculous book—the Bible—has become our instructions for living. As A. W. Tozer (1897-1963) reminds us, "The Holy Scriptures tell us what we could never learn any other way; they tell us what we are, who we are, how we got here, why we are here and what we are required to do while we remain here."[8] We can learn a lot from reading the Bible—God's instruction book. We can learn even more by *practicing* what we read.

The Bible is for men as they are, but God wants us to become more than we now are. We must never forget that while other books were given for our information, the Bible was given for our transformation. The Bible takes the guesswork out of living, for it gives us governing principles, guidelines, and an infusion of divine life. The Bible is like a compass—it always points the believer in the right direction.

This divine book also shares guidelines for the release of joy. Joy is a powerful emotion that needs channeling to keep it from being destructive. Producing and channeling our joy, the Bible also gives us guidelines for releasing joy. It teaches us, *"O clap your hands, all ye people; shout unto God with the voice of triumph"* (Psalm 47:1). Seventeen times throughout Scripture we are told, *"...sing praise to the LORD God of Israel."* We are encouraged to dance before the Lord and to testify of His goodness to us here in the land of the living. We are exhorted to raise our hands and to laugh as a release of the great joy God has inspired in our lives.

God does not propose special "religious" expressions of our joy. He just encourages us to release our joy unto Him. Perhaps a closer observation of how sports fans react when their team is winning will give us an even broader comprehension of how to express our joy unto the Lord. We have but one set of emotions. "Religion" tends to suppress the release of those emotions, but God loves His children and is pleased with any honest expression of joy.

It is sad that religion has equated silence with reverence. "Let's have a moment of silent prayer," is an oft-repeated phrase in religious circles, and calling for a "moment of silence" is considered a reverent act by thousands outside the church. You would be hard-pressed to substantiate that in the Scriptures, however. True, the prophet said, *"But the LORD is in his holy temple: let all the earth keep silence before him"* (Habakkuk 2:20). This is in the Bible once, and I believe every Christian should do it once; but hundreds of times we are told to shout unto the Lord, to sing unto God, to play musical instruments before Him, and to dance hilariously before Him. Jubilation, not introspective silence, is the Bible's projection for response to God. After all, God came in human flesh to induce great joy, not to produce depressing guilt. I think you will find that the Bible illustrates or supports almost any honorable form of releasing joy.

There is still another way the Bible supports joy in our lives. It is both the source and sustenance of our spiritual life. Jesus (the Living Word) and the Bible (the written Word) are quite inseparable, and both are pictured as the manna that God provided in the wilderness. We must feed on Jesus in order for our spirits to live and grow, and we do that by reading, meditating on, and spiritually ingesting His Word.

When our circumstances seem to turn totally negative, we can find positive joy in reading and applying the Bible. Circumstances are temporal; God's Word is eternal. David knew this, for he wrote, *"Sing unto the LORD, O ye saints of his, and give thanks at the remembrance of his holiness. For his anger endureth but a moment; in his favour is life: weeping may endure for a night, but joy cometh in the morning"* (Psalm 30:4-5).

Why does this work so well? Perhaps A.W. Tozer explained it when he said, "The sacred page is not meant to be the end, but only the means toward the end, which is knowing God himself."[9] If the Bible does not bring us before the throne of God, we have failed in our reading. The Bible is a glorious revelation of God's purposes, provisions, promises, and person. If we let the Bible direct us to the person of God, we will discover that He has an invisible kingdom at work right here on the earth.

For Reflection

1. If God and the Bible are truly inseparable, why are some Bible students so morbid and joyless?
2. List some ways the Bible gives for the expression of our joy.
3. The joyful book offers joyful promises. List six promises you find in the Bible that produce joy in you.

Endnotes

1. *Draper's Book of Quotations for the Christian World*, Edythe Draper, Copyright © 1992, Tyndale House Publishers, Inc., Wheaten, IL.
2. Ibid., Entry 644.
3. Ibid., Entry 752.
4. Martyn Lloyd-Jones, *Leadership*, Vol. 8, No. 3.
5. Don Lyon, *Leadership*, Vol. 5, No. 1
6. Entry 733, *Draper's Book of Quotations for the Christian World*, Edythe Draper, Copyright © 1992, Tyndale House Publishers, Inc., Wheaten, IL.
7. *The Speaker's Sourcebook*, pg. 32, Entry 655. Copyright © 1960 by Zondervan Publishing House, Grand Rapids, MI.
8. A.W. Tozer, Entry 735—*Draper's Book of Quotations for the Christian World*, Edythe Draper, Copyright © 1992, Tyndale House Publishers, Inc., Wheaten, IL
9. Ibid., A.W. Tozer, Entry 743.

6

Joy and God's Kingdom

"Shouts of joy and victory resound in the tents of the righteous: 'The Lord's right hand has done mighty things!'" (Psalm 118:15, NIV).

The interruption of the telephone pulled me away from my computer as a pastor asked me a question about an incident in the Old Testament. In the course of our conversation, he told me that some years ago he was offered an opportunity to have the author of the chorus *Hallelujah!* (that Katherine Kuhlman popularized) as a guest musician on Sunday morning. The pastor said, "I was shocked when he walked into the church. He was a hippie—long hair, clothes, and all. The shock was so spontaneous I couldn't change my expression before the young man noticed it."

"That's all right," he said. "Everyone is shocked the first time they see me."

"Are you really the one who wrote the beautiful *Hallelujah!* chorus?" the pastor asked.

"The one and only," the musician answered with a smile.

"Then why don't you cut your hair and put on a suit?"

"Because God has challenged me to shock His people out of their religious comfort zones," the musician replied.

"He succeeded in his ministry that morning," the pastor assured me.

Isn't it likely that God had a similar goal for John the Baptist? He was alarming enough with his camel hair tunic that was fastened with a leather belt and with his diet of locusts and wild honey (see Matthew 3:4), but his message was as shocking as his way of life. *"Repent ye: for the kingdom of heaven is at hand"* (Matthew 3:2). His proclamation was unlike anything the people had ever heard. Many prophets in the Old Testament had called for repentance, both personal and national, but never had anyone dared proclaim that *"the kingdom of heaven is at hand."* It is likely that his anxious listeners questioned, "What is the kingdom of heaven?"

When Jesus came on the scene, He was as unlike John as silk is from sackcloth. He was so like other Jewish men that He could hide in a crowd by just standing still; yet He, too, seemed to have an alarming message, *"The time is fulfilled, and the kingdom of God is at hand: repent ye, and believe the gospel"* (Mark 1:15). The phrase *kingdom of God* occurs 14 times in Mark, 32 times in Luke, but only 4 times in Matthew. In its place, Matthew substitutes *kingdom of heaven.* This was probably an accommodation of the Jews' aversion to using the name of God. Most scholars see these two terms as interchangeable—it is one kingdom with two designations.

His Kingdom

The Greek word translated "kingdom" is *basileia* which means "rule or a kingdom." It is used in the absolute and the abstract sense of the word. It may depict a future rule or a present rule; a future realm or a present realm. Eschatology and history combine in *basileia,* which could create a rather confusing picture here in the Gospels.

> When Jesus began to preach the gospel of the kingdom, He already knew His vocation to be its Founder and its Lord…Jesus is not simply the Founder of this kingdom, but it is *His* kingdom as well as the Father's, and He is Lord and King over it…If Jesus was from the first fully conscious of Himself as the Son of God and Founder of this kingdom, this kingdom in His view could not have been a mere *future* thing, but must have been conceived of as *already existing.* [1]

This theme of God's kingdom consumed Jesus. In Him, the great future had already become "present time." He preached the reality of God's kingdom everywhere He went. He told stories about it, gave illustrative parables about it, declared that it was both present and coming, and placed Himself as the King in God's kingdom. Feeling that wherever the King was, the kingdom was, Jesus commissioned His disciples, *"And as ye go, preach, saying, The kingdom of heaven is at hand"* (Matthew 10:7). *"The king is here"* was the theme of the disciples.

One God: One Kingdom

Still, Jesus saw a far higher picture of the kingdom than His earthly visit, for when the disciples asked for a model prayer, Jesus said, *"After this manner therefore pray ye: Our Father which art in heaven, Hallowed be thy name. Thy kingdom come. Thy will be done in earth, as it is in heaven"* (Matthew 6:9-10). We are to pray that the rule of God in heaven be equaled here on earth—one God, one kingdom.

Few people in John the Baptist's gatherings had so much as a clue to what was meant by *"the kingdom of God,"* and probably not too many who followed Jesus comprehended it either.

Christ's disciples and most of His followers interpreted *"the kingdom of God"* to mean the overthrow of the Roman domination of Palestine and a return to self-rule. Either they were wrong or Jesus failed in His mission: Rome's worst acts of occupation occurred after the ascension of Jesus.

Is the concept of God's kingdom any more understood by modern believers than by the disciples? The Jews erred in their concept of this kingdom, expecting a political reign of Jesus. It is likely that modern Christians err in viewing the Church as the kingdom of God. It isn't. Robert Schuller, speaking of the Lord's prayer, said, "God's kingdom is everywhere. God is the Father, the Church is the mother."[2]

In his most recent book, *Future Worship*, LaMar Boschman wrote:

> I believe the Church is the Bride of Christ. But I also agree with Charles Simpson who said, "The church is Christ's Bride, but she's not His whole life!" Godly men cherish, honor and enjoy their wives. We would die for them. However a quick survey of a man's life will reveal that a relatively small portion of his work and pursuits are concentrated on his wife. The Church's collision course with reality is a reflection of her illusion that she is His whole life. *The Kingdom of God is His life. She's His wife.*[3]

The Church by Itself Is Not the Kingdom

The kingdom of God is far bigger than God's Church. The Church is *part* of His kingdom, but it is not synonymous with the kingdom! Brother Boschman reminds us,

> Wisdom has never remained (or, at times, ever even showed up) in the Church. God has never confined Himself to our thoughts—even our "religious" thoughts (*especially* our religious thoughts). The image of the Church as a gatekeeper for anything and everything important has no basis in fact, Scripture or history. His kingdom is much more grand and majestic than the Church.[4]

What, then, is the kingdom of God? The theologian of a past century said: "The kingdom is in its beginnings...the introduction of *a new principle of divine rule* into the hearts of men, through the word (Matthew 13:19), the truth (John 18:37), the Spirit (John 3:5-6), in virtue of which, changed in disposition (Matthew 18:3) they become doers of the will of the Father in heaven (Matthew 7:21)."[5]

John Hess-Yoder gives us an interesting picture:

> While serving as a missionary in Laos, I discovered an illustration of the kingdom of God. Before the colonialists imposed national boundaries, the kings of Laos and Vietnam reached an agreement on taxation in the border areas. Those who ate short-grain rice, built their houses on stilts, and decorated them with Indian-style serpents were considered Laotians. On the other hand, those who ate long-grain rice, built their houses on the ground, and decorated them with Chinese-style dragons were considered Vietnamese. The exact location of a person's home was not what determined his or her nationality. Instead, each person belonged to the kingdom whose cultural values he or she exhibited. So it is with us: we live in the world, but as part of God's kingdom, we are to live according to his kingdom's standards and values.[6]

When the beloved apostle Paul wrote his theological treatise to the church at Rome, he dared enter into the discussion about the kingdom of God. He wrote: *"For the kingdom of God is not a matter of eating and drinking, but of righteousness, peace and joy in the Holy Spirit"* (Romans 14:17, NIV). Paul did not view God's kingdom as geographic, political, or even religious. He refused to see the kingdom manifested in possessions, positions, power, or even people. He defined God's reign throughout all of creation as, *"righteousness, peace, and joy in the Holy Spirit."*

Characteristics of the Kingdom

Paul seemed to say that the kingdom of God is an extension of the nature of God. God and His kingdom are inseparable! When Ezra lay before the Lord confessing the sins of the remnant in the land, he cried, *"O LORD God of Israel, thou art righteous!" (Ezra 9:15a).* Isaiah called Jesus, *"the Prince of Peace"* (Isaiah 9:6). When Jesus voiced His High Priestly prayer to the Father, He asked, *"...that they may have the full measure of my joy within them"* (John 17:13b, NIV). Righteousness, peace, and joy are all inherent in the nature of our God, and they are the fundamental characteristics of the kingdom of God.

Most New Testament believers fully accept the first two definitions of God's kingdom—*righteousness and peace,* but many have failed to realize that the kingdom of God is inherent *joy.* Religion has a rather consistent tendency to squeeze joy out of living in God's kingdom. It attempts to legislate righteousness and demands peace, and yet neither of these can be achieved by our Christian discipline or fervent religious activities. The harder we try to produce righteousness and peace, the less we seem to have them. No wonder religious zealots have so little joy. Righteousness and peace cannot be achieved by works. They come exclusively by faith in Christ Jesus. They are part of the essential nature of God and we cannot produce God; we can merely receive Him.

While this almost seems self-evident, many religious persons fail to realize that joy is also part of the essential nature of God. The true secret of joy is that it is found in God and can only be received from God. He is its source, and He also becomes its object.

The singers sang in the Messianic Psalm, *"Your throne, O God, will last for ever and ever; a scepter of justice will be the scepter of your kingdom. You love righteousness and hate wickedness; therefore God, your God, has set you above your companions by anointing you with the oil of joy"* (Psalm 45:6-7, NIV). God copiously anointed His Son Jesus with *"the oil of joy."* Wouldn't you think He wants to do similarly with His *"many sons"* He is bringing into glory (Hebrews 2:10)?

Jesus taught us that the route into the kingdom of God is to repent. The removal of sin is a prerequisite to the possession of righteousness, peace, and divine joy. It is the step that takes us out of our self-centered realm into the reign of Christ Jesus. God has promised to respond to true confession of sin with forgiveness— *"If we confess our sins, he is faithful and just and will forgive us our sins and purify us from all unrighteousness"* (1 John 1:9, NIV). God does not merely respond to our repentance by forgiving us our sins and then releasing us to produce joy for living. He lovingly anoints us with the oil of joy. He shares His joyous nature with us. He offers to let us be joyful in Him.

In the past few years, there has been a proliferation of preaching on directing our faith to acquire wealth and possessions so we can be happy in life. Evelyn Bence, who has edited some of my books, writes: "An English visitor recently commented about U.S. churches. 'You Americans are so concerned about being happy,' as if our kingdoms were the focal point of God's designs rather than God's kingdom the focal point of ours."[7] The work of God's grace does not have our happiness as a central theme. It offers something far superior to fleeting happiness; it has God's joy at its very core.

"Wherever God rules over the human heart as King, there is the kingdom of God established."[8] Furthermore, wherever God's kingdom is established, God's joy remains supreme. Little wonder, then, that Christ's consistent teaching was on the kingdom of God. This universal kingdom of God is our gateway to the joy of the Lord in everyday living.

Until we are members of God's reign, we really have no access to His abiding presence. Isn't it most unlikely, then, that we will find joy in God's presence until we have found the joy of His kingdom? When we surrender to His reign, we become aware of His imperishable presence. What security, peace, and joy this brings to our lives.

For Reflection

1. What three qualities did Paul declare were foundational to the kingdom of God?
2. Psalm 45 declares that God anointed Jesus with oil. Which kind of oil was this?
3. What steps must you take to successfully relate to and participate in the kingdom of God?
4. What does it mean to surrender to the reign of God?

Endnotes

1. James Hastings, M.A., D.D., *A Dictionary of the Bible*, pg. 849, 851, Copyright © 1899, T&T Clark, Edinburgh, Scotland.
2. Robert Schuller's *Hour of Power*, Broadcast #1517.
3. LaMar Boschman, *Future Worship*, pg. 7, Copyright © 1999, LaMar Boschman. Printed by Renew Books, Venture, CA.
4. Ibid., Chapter 10.
5. James Hastings, M.A., D.D., *A Dictionary of the Bible*, pg. 852, Copyright © 1899, T&T Clark, Edinburgh, Scotland.
6. John Hess-Yoder, *Leadership*, Vol. 7, No.3, Portland, Oregon.
7. Evelyn Bence in *Christian Herald* (April 1987), *Christianity Today*, Vol. 31, No. 10, pg. 46.
8. Paul W. Harrison, Entry 4736—*Draper's Book of Quotations for the Christian World*, Edythe Draper, Copyright © 1992, Tyndale House Publishers, Inc., Wheaton, IL.

7

Joy and God's Presence

"They ate and drank with great joy in the presence of the Lord that day..." (1 Chronicles 29:22, NIV).

David, who lived many generations before the proclamation of the kingdom of God, had learned the secret of being joyful. He wrote, *"Thou wilt shew me the path of life; in thy presence is fulness of joy, at thy right hand are pleasures for evermore"* (Psalm 16:11). He had discovered that joy is inseparable from the presence of God. It always has been—ask Adam and Eve; and it always will be—reread the book of Revelation.

Because Peter quoted Psalm 16 on the day of Pentecost as applicable to Jesus, commentators usually connect verse 11 with the resurrection of Jesus and the great joy He experienced when He was reunited with His Father in heaven.

The personal application the commentators make is an assurance that we, too, will know ultimate joy in heaven. One of them wrote: "Joy unalloyed, complete, enduring, is not for this world. Not possible where all fairest flowers fade, fruits wither, brightest days have their sunset, fountains run dry. There will be many sources of 'everlasting joy' in the heavenly life; society, deliverance from pain, grief, sin, conflict, etc., but the source of all, *'the fountain of living waters'* (Jeremiah 2:13) will be God's presence."[1]

Will be God's presence? Didn't Jesus promise *"living water"* as a present reality to the woman at the well (John 4:10)? God is not going to be *"the fountain of living waters"* at some future date. His presence *is* a fountain of living water, whether we touch that presence in eternity or in time.

My heart says "Hallelujah!" to making Psalm 16 a Messianic Psalm, but my spirit wonders if this passage may illustrate a prophetic perspective, in which it has an immediate and a future fulfillment. I don't believe this Psalm is entirely futuristic. It does, indeed, apply to Jesus, but there is every reason to believe that it also applies to us and to the psalmist who penned it.

Matthew Henry wrote, "Christ being the Head of the body, the church, these verses may, for the most part, be applied to all Christians, guided and animated by the Spirit of Christ; and we may hence learn…that if our eyes be ever toward God, our hearts and tongues may ever rejoice in Him."[2]

This great British commentator makes my point for me. I don't dispute the ultimate joy that awaits us in heaven, but Psalm 16:11 promises us, "*You have let me experience the joys of life and the exquisite pleasures of your own eternal presence*" (TLB). John Knox translated verse 16 in this way: "*Thou wilt shew me the way of life, make me full of gladness in thy presence; at thy right hand are delights that will endure forever.*" James Moffatt gives us a slightly different flavor: "*thou wilt reveal the path to life, to the full joy of thy presence; to the bliss of being close to thee forever.*"

In God's presence is perfect joy—"*fulness of joy,*" "*exquisite pleasures,*" "*delights that will endure,*" "*the bliss of being close to thee.*" When Peter quoted this verse, he said, "*…you will fill me with joy in your presence*" (Acts 2:28, NIV), and this joy is available today.

The Joy of Living in His Presence

As the Bible is fuller than all other books of human life, so you can nowhere match the fullness and variety of its images of joy. Besides its warm Eastern pictures, our Western modern life looks bleak and sad. Above the whole range of common life, it opens the range of *spiritual* joy—the joy of forgiveness, of salvation, of knowledge, of trust, peace, security, of fellowship with God in Christ…Higher still the Scripture lifts our thought—to the joy of angels; to God's own joy.[3]

The timing for entering into this "*fulness of joy*" is when we are in "*thy presence.*" To Moses, God's presence was a present reality, for God had promised him, "*My Presence will go with you, and I will give you rest*"

(Exodus 33:14, NIV). Moses' response to God was, "*If your Presence does not go with us, do not send us up from here*" (Verse 15).

God's presence was life itself to King David, for he exclaimed, "*Surely the righteous shall give thanks unto thy name: the upright shall dwell in thy presence*" (Psalm 140:13, emphasis added). When David was convicted for his sin of adultery, he cried to God, "*Cast me not away from thy presence...Restore unto me the joy of thy salvation*" (Psalm 51:11-12*a*). To David, God's presence and His joy were inseparable.

At the end of Christ's ministry, when He gave the Great Commission to His disciples, He assured them, "*I am with you always even to the end of the world.*" (Matthew 28:20, *TLB*). Paul put this assurance as part of the great mystery of the Church, for he wrote, "*Christ in you, the hope of glory*" (Colossians 1:27*b*, NIV).

We have the assurance of God's presence in the prophetic Psalms, the poetic Psalms, the words of Jesus, and the writings of Paul. Logically then, if we have access to His *presence* in the here and now, surely we have access to His *joy* in our present experience. Peter wrote, "*Though you have not seen him, you love him; and even though you do not see him now, you believe in him and are filled with an inexpressible and glorious joy*" (1 Peter 1:8, NIV).

Paul blessed the Church in Rome with this benediction: "*May the God of hope fill you with all joy and peace as you trust in him...*" (Romans 15:13, *NIV*). This cannot be seen as a future experience. It is a present reality. Similarly, Jesus made His joy available to His disciples while He was still here on the earth. We read, "*...I say these things while I am still in the world, so that they may have the full measure of my joy within them*" (John 17:13, NIV). He even said that God would answer our prayer sent up from the earth to enhance our joy—"*...ask, and ye shall receive, that your joy may be full*" (John 16:24).

Two things are immediately obvious from this. First, Jesus wants us to have full and complete joy. Second, God's presence is available in our time/space dimension, and when we are consciously in His presence, we will enjoy a divine joy and gladness beyond anything that we have ever experienced. This has been the testimony of the great saints of the ages. It was also testimony of many martyrs as the flames consumed their bodies or the lions tore them apart in the arena. God's presence so filled them with joy that they were able to praise and worship God with their last breath.

The Practical Aspect

Please don't think that the hustle and bustle of our modern life has changed this. We have changed, but God says, *"I am the LORD, I change not"* (Malachi 3:6a). God's availability and the joy of His presence are constants in the spiritual world, as dependable as night and day. We don't have to plead for His presence; we simply acknowledge it, appropriate it, and apply it. When we do, we experience God's fountain of joy bubbling in our spirit.

"But," you say, "this is only provisional. It isn't practical."

You are correct is saying that it is provisional. All these assurances of God's presence in our current experiences are promises. They are divine promises—promises made by God, and God has a reputation of keeping every word He speaks. Paul assures us, *"For no matter how many promises God has made, they are 'Yes' in Christ. And so through him the 'Amen' is spoken by us to the glory of God"* (2 Corinthians 1:20, NIV).

There is often a gap between God's promises and their performance, and it is our job to fill that gap. The promises are conditional—"I will, if you will." Quite honestly, we live most of our day unaware of God's presence. The noises of life crowd out His "still, small voice," and the emotions connected with our daily activity displace the joy His presence would bring to us. Intellectually we know that God is near, but experientially, God might as well be in another galaxy.

What can we do to claim these promises and awaken our consciousness to God's nearness? How can we experience the intense joy of His presence in day-to-day living? I think the worship book of the Bible, the Book of Psalms, actually holds solid clues for us.

Our Point of Entrance

Does anything in life make us more aware of another's presence than talking with him or her? David cried, *"May my prayer be set before you like incense; may the lifting up of my hands be like the evening sacrifice"*

(Psalm 141:2, NIV). Sacrifice and incense was the Old Testament approach to God, but David with prophetic insight said he offered *prayer* as both sacrifice and incense. He found a way into God's realized presence through prayer.

So have many of us since his time. Personally, prayer is my number one entrance point to God's presence. As I talk with Him, I become aware of His immediate presence, and the joy of His Person floods my soul. I may have approached Him with my personal burdens, but after conversing with Him, the burdens are exchanged for "joy unspeakable and full of glory."

An unnamed psalmist offers another avenue for becoming aware of God's presence. He says, "*Let us come before his presence with thanksgiving, and make a joyful noise unto him with psalms*" (Psalm 95:2). Thanksgiving, jubilation, and God's Word are certified routes into God's presence. We all are prone to rush into God's presence with petitions rather than with thanksgiving; however, this only burdens us with a consciousness of ourselves and our problems. When we begin prayer time instead by thanking God, we make ourselves think of *Him*, bringing an awareness of His person and His presence.

Similarly, we can actually open ourselves to receive His joy. Doing this with Psalms, daring to quote God's Word back to Him, makes this entrance into His presence even more powerful. In my book, *Praying the Scriptures*, I say, "When we let the Bible become our prayer, we are praying an inspired vocabulary. It will often release deep inner feelings far better than extemporized prayers that will come from our minds."[4]

Still another psalmist instructs us to, "*Serve the LORD with gladness: come before his presence with singing*" (Psalm 100:2). That first phrase is particularly important because when we serve the Lord with sadness or reluctance, we are in His disfavor. In fact, one of the reasons God gave for sending Israel into captivity and privation was, "*Because you did not serve the LORD your God joyfully and gladly in the time of prosperity*" (Deuteronomy 28:47, NIV). Could that still be His attitude toward us? Serving the Lord is supposed to be joyful and fun-filled.

"Come before His presence with singing," the worshiper calls to us. Singing both releases our emotions and opens us to God's great emotion of joy. Furthermore, singing songs gives us a tailor-made vocabulary to express our emotions to God. If this were not enough, the book of Revelation supplies proof that heaven is filled with music and songs. The singing of praises is an acceptable response to the presence of God, but even more than that, **it is a guaranteed route into God's presence.**

We need to realize that none of these actions produce the presence of God. God is among His people. These responses to God merely help us become aware of His presence. The joy of His presence is around us at all times, but our conscious minds are far too seldom aware of Him. When I turn my attention from the inward look to the upward look, I become aware of God and begin to share in His glorious joy.

There are wondrous occasions when God simply imposes His presence upon us. We often call these "sovereign visitations" or "revivals." Our initial response to the presence of this Holy God is usually repentance, but once forgiveness is accepted, unbridled joy follows. Look at the laughter the Toronto visitation brought to believers. The early Pentecostals were sometimes called "holy rollers" because they could not handle the great joy God's presence brought them but would roll on the floor in laughter and tears.

When God's presence is realized, we are filled with *"joy unspeakable and full of glory"* (1 Peter 1:8*b*). The Living Bible translates this verse, *"...you are happy with the inexpressible joy that comes from heaven itself."*

When we are in God's presence and inundated with heaven's joy, we must find a way to express that joy or we will burst. Our joy becomes absolutely glorious and heavenly rejoicing.

For Reflection

1. Psalm 16:11 capsulizes the Bible's theology of joy. Why is there joy in His presence?
2. If God's presence is available in our time/space dimension, must we await Christ's return to enjoy God's joy?
3. List three things we can do to become aware of God's presence.
4. Ask Him to remind you to do those things throughout each day.

Endnotes

1. Joseph S. Exell, *The Pulpit Commentary*, pg. 100, Copyright © 1950, Wm. B. Eerdmans Publishing Company, Grand Rapids, MI.

2. Matthew Henry, *Commentary on the Holy Bible*, pg. 118. Copright © 1979 by Thomas Nelson Inc., Publishers, Nashville, TN.

3. Joseph S. Exell, *The Pulpit Commentary*, pg. 99, Copyright © 1950, Wm. B. Eerdmans Publishing Company, Grand Rapids, MI.

4. Judson Cornwall, *Praying the Scriptures*, pg. 11, Copyright © 1990, Creation House, Lake Mary, FL.

Section 2

The Characteristics of Joy

8

Joy Is a Gift

"You have filled my heart with greater joy than when their grain and new wine abound" (Psalm 4:7, NIV).

In the first division of this book, I have pointed out that the very source of joy is God, as revealed in the Trinity, the Bible, and God's presence. Every one of these avenues through which divine joy flows is declared to be a gift of God.

Consider Jesus as the source of joy. Very likely the first Scripture verse you memorized was John 3:16. It unequivocally declares, *"For God so loved the world, that he gave his only begotten Son, that whosoever believeth in him should not perish, but have everlasting life."* God gave Jesus, and tells us in His Word that Jesus is the provider of everlasting life. We see two wonderful sources of joy here: the Living Word and the written Word.

In light of this, how people can read the Bible and see nothing but condemnation and wrath escapes me. "The glum, sour faces of many Christians ...They rather give the impression that instead of coming from the Father's joyful banquet, they have just come from the sheriff who has auctioned off their sins and now are sorry they can't get them back again."[1] The Bible is a book of release, redemption, restoration, and joy. Would God give us anything less than that?

A Voluntary and Priceless Gift

Another important point is made by Paul regarding these gifts. He reminds us that not only did God give His Son **to** us, Jesus deliberately gave Himself **for** us. *"Who gave himself for us, that he might redeem us from all iniquity, and purify unto himself a peculiar people, zealous of* *good works*" (Titus 2:14). Paul also said of Jesus, "*Who gave himself for our sins, that he might deliver us from this present evil world, according to the will of God and our Father*" (Galatians 1:4). If this gift of Jesus doesn't induce great joy into our lives, nothing else will—"If the angels in heaven rejoice and shout when a person gives his life to Christ why should we be denied the same joy?"[2]

We have seen that not only is Jesus a source of divine joy, but the Holy Spirit—a gift from God to us—is also a source of our joy because He is part of the Godhead. When talking to the woman at the well, "*Jesus answered her, 'If you knew the gift of God and who it is that asks you for a drink, you would have asked him and he would have given you living water*'" (John 4:10, NIV). He clearly connected the "living water" with the gift of God. Hold that thought for a moment, and note what Peter said in his sermon on the day of Pentecost, "*Repent and be baptized, every one of you, in the name of Jesus Christ for the forgiveness of your sins. And you will receive the gift of the Holy Spirit*" (Acts 2:38, NIV).

Charles Spurgeon, that great English preacher of the past century, wrote the following:

> The great King, immortal, invisible, the divine person called the Holy Ghost, the Holy Spirit: it is he that quickens the soul, or else it would lie dead forever; it is he that makes it tender, or else it would never feel; it is he that imparts efficacy to the Word preached, or else it could never reach farther than the ear; it is he who breaks the heart; it is he who makes it whole.[3]

What holy joy this effects in us!

We cannot overstate the key role the Holy Spirit plays in bringing God's joy to our lives. Oswald Chambers said, "Call the comforter by the term you think best—Advocate, Helper, Paraclete, the word conveys the indefinable blessedness of his sympathy, an inward invisible kingdom that causes the saint to sing through every night of sorrow. This Holy Comforter represents the ineffable motherhood of God."[4] What a gift God has given to us, and what a joy producer this gift has become to believers worldwide!

We have already mentioned that the Bible is a gift from God to us. The psalmist said, "*He sent his word, and healed them, and delivered them from their destructions"* (Psalm 107:20). We did not earn the Bible or even deserve it. God *sent* it to us. Jesus clearly coupled His spoken words with the reception of joy when He told His disciples, *"These things have I spoken unto you, that my joy might remain in you, and that your joy might be full"* (John 15:11).

"God the Father is the giver of Holy Scripture, God the Son is the theme of Holy Scripture; and God the Spirit is the author, authenticator, and interpreter of Holy Scripture."[5] The Bible absolutely overflows with the joy of the Godhead.

Even the blessed kingdom of God that is also a source of our joy is described by Jesus as a gift: *"Fear not, little flock; for it is your Father's good pleasure to give you the kingdom"* (Luke 12:32). The very nature of this kingdom is *"righteousness, and peace, and joy in the Holy Ghost"* according to Romans 14:17. The book of Revelation describes the kingdom as filled with praises, shouts, dances, and celebrations of joy. We need not wait for the complete fulfillment of God's kingdom to be joyful. I can promise you that whatever measure we can enter into will fill us with more joy than we know how to handle.

"Freely You Have Received"

If every source of God's joy is a gift from God, and not something we have earned, we have no excuse for living without a bubbling joy in our hearts. The reason for lack of joy must lie in our unwillingness to accept this free gift from God.

Not only is the source of joy a gift, but the cause for joy is equally a divine gratuity to us. There was no chance for real joy when we lived under the burden of guilt and condemnation for sin, but while, *"the wages of sin is death; . . . the gift of God is eternal life through Jesus Christ our Lord"* (Romans 6:23). Also, *"For by grace are ye saved through faith; and that not of yourselves: it is the gift of God"* (Ephesians 2:8). We dare not underestimate this gift, for it is the foundation upon which our renewed relationship with God is built. Sin separated us from God and hid His face from us. (See Isaiah 59:2.) Jesus took our place that we might have His love, joy, and peace. He took our sin that we might have His salvation.

God's free gift of salvation settled the sin question once and for all. By doing so, it renewed our fellowship with God. If you have forgotten the great joy of your salvation, get around a new convert. Not long ago in Dayton, Ohio, Pastor Patrick Murray and his wife Jackie met me at the airport and took me directly to a restaurant for something to eat. In chit-chatting with the waitress, she said she might come to church the next day to hear me preach. She did come and subsequently responded to the altar call following the second service. She gave her heart to Jesus and was both saved and filled with the Holy Spirit. You should have seen her. Her face lit up with a smile, her eyes danced with delight, and she could hardly talk for crying and laughing so much.

Abundant and Overflowing Joy

When the weight of sin is lifted and the reality of forgiveness dawns upon the heart, joy flows abundantly. Tears and laughter intermingle as a new convert tries to express his or her changed inner feelings. Unless religious people burden the new convert with rules, regulations, and religious activities, he or she may float on an emotional high for weeks, so great is the joy of salvation in Jesus Christ.

All these sources for joy are direct gifts from Father God to His children. Not only that, but one of the characteristics of joy is that joy, in itself, is a gift from God. Solomon, the wise man of the Old Testament, knew this. Out of his depth of experience he wrote, *"For God giveth to a man that is good in his sight wisdom, and knowledge, and joy"* (Ecclesiastes 2:26a).

James also insisted, *"Every good and perfect gift is from above, coming down from the Father of the heavenly lights, who does not change like shifting shadows"* (James 1:17, NIV). God is a giving Father, not a mercenary merchant.

His favorite way to impart His joy is to invite us into His presence. He revealed this to David, who then wrote, *"You have made known to me the path of life; you will fill me with joy in your presence, with eternal pleasures at your right hand"* (Psalm 16:11, NIV).

My little dog, Deacon, daily illustrates this to me. His joy is not in his food dish or in his toys; his joy is in me. He runs in circles when I come into the house, and usually beats me to my chair to crawl onto my lap. His joy is complete when he can be with me. Similarly, the presence of the

Lord, whether touched in prayer, praise, worship, or in reading the Scriptures, fills us with rapture and inexpressible joy. The joy is in being with Him.

Dr. Stelman Smith, with whom I wrote the book *The Exhaustive Dictionary of Bible Names*, graciously acted as a consultant on this book project. He emailed me the following comment about joy, to which my spirit says, "Amen!"

> For me, God's joy is the intense awareness of His presence in my life in the middle of "ANYTHING" that touches my life. Joy is not just a feeling, but life expression from God that gives complete inner peace (lack of inner conflict = joy). That tremendous peace of God, the presence of His love to keep me, then becomes the source of my strength and I can then rejoice in the victory He has given, knowing that inner awareness of His abiding presence (JOY) that will strengthen me in any circumstance.

Our Joy in Jesus and the Holy Spirit

In the Gospels, Jesus was the source of joy for the disciples. Before leaving them through death, resurrection, and ascension, Jesus explained what was about to happen and said, *"I have told you this so that my joy may be in you and that your joy may be complete"* (John 15:11, NIV). *The Message* translation says this: *"I've told you these things for a purpose: that my joy might be your joy, and your joy wholly mature."*

Just a few verses later He added, *"When the Counselor comes, whom I will send to you from the Father, the Spirit of truth who goes out from the Father, he will testify about me"* (John 15:26). Although it was necessary for Jesus to leave the disciples bodily, He did not abandon them. He sent His Spirit to dwell in the disciples—becoming in them what Christ had been to them on the earth. Relationship with Jesus in bodily form had been the source of joy for the disciples. Now relationship to the Holy Spirit who would dwell within them would be their source of divine joy.

Our joy will not be found in activity—even religious activity. It is found in relationship with God through the Holy Spirit. It is sad to me that so many believers view the very means of receiving divine joy as boring

Christian duty. Bible reading, prayer, and attendance at worship services are far more than Christian disciplines. They are the very channels of entering into God's presence where the fullness of joy abounds. They help to mature and maintain our joy in the Lord.

Unquestionably, joy is a gift from God. It is received in faith as are all gifts from God. He freely offers this gift, but explains that His joy cannot be received apart from His presence.

Perhaps our loss of joy can be attributed to the small amount of time we invest in God's presence. We usually spend more time in the presence of our television set—which invites persons into our front rooms who we wouldn't even allow past our front door—than we spend in the presence of God. One reason this happens is that we Americans confuse amusement with joy. We forget that the word "muse" means to think, while the prefix "a" makes a negative out of the word. Hence, "amuse" really means *to not think*. This may offer temporary relief from stress and the pain of life, but it isn't even close to the joy of life that God's presence brings to us.

There is another great contrast between amusement and joy. The former is short-lived and must be repeated, while the latter is perpetual. Hallelujah!

For Reflection
1. If joy is indeed a gift from God, why are so few Christians truly joyful?
2. What was the source of joy for Christ's disciples?
3. List four or more sources of joy you can tap into at will. Do you regularly reach for these? If not, *why* not?

Endnotes
1. J.I. Packer, as quoted in Edythe Draper, *Draper's Book of Quotations for the Christian World*, Entry 655, Copyright © 1992 by Tyndale House Publishers, Inc., Wheaton, IL.
2. Raleigh Washington, *Leadership*, Vol. 11, No. 1.
3. Charles Haddon Spurgeon (1834-1892) as quoted in Edythe

Draper, *Draper's Book of Quotations for the Christian World*, Entry 5794.

4. Ibid., Oswald Chambers, Entry 5775.

5. Helmut Tielicke, *Leadership*, Vol. 1, No. 4.

9

Joy Is Perpetual

"...everlasting joy will crown their heads..." (Isaiah 35:10, NIV).

Joy is not distinguished merely by being a gift, although that aspect is something for which we are profoundly grateful. An even stronger characteristic of joy is its perpetuity. Unlike happiness, which comes and goes with happenings, joy comes to stay. Happiness requires beneficial circumstances. Bad happenings induce sorrow or sadness. Contrasted to this, joy has its source in another life, another world, and another Being. Our joy has its roots in God and His eternal kingdom. Earthly happenings cannot touch it, human emotions cannot drown it out, and Satanic intervention finds it so secure that it cannot be destroyed.

I observed this characteristic of joy in the life of my mother. Saddled with the responsibility of five children, living through the depression years, active with Dad in the ministry of pioneering small churches, Mother had circumstances that offered few happy times. Money was in very short supply, and her generous and compassionate heart urged her to share what little she had with others who had even less. The entire family dressed in hand-me-downs and pass-them-ons. I repeatedly overheard Mother interceding with God for enough food to feed the family another meal.

To add to this, Mother was seldom in good health, and my parents could not often afford medical help. Yet Mother possessed an exuberance of joy that infected everyone around her. To her dying day, she maintained that divine joy. She was a praying woman who had touched eternity's joy and was simply sustained by that joy at all times. Through it, she developed a sense of humor that helped her and the entire family through tough times.

As I look back on my childhood, I would not trade the joy that my mother provided in our family for all the natural things we lacked if in having them we had to sacrifice that joy. The things we lacked were temporal; the joy we had was eternal.

The Bible clearly tells us that when we close our eyes in death or when the Lord returns for us, *"God shall wipe away all tears from their eyes; and there shall be no more death, neither sorrow, nor crying, neither shall there be any more pain: for the former things are passed away"* (Revelation 21:4, emphasis mine). "Of course," you say, "because nothing lasts forever." Wrong! The Bible is full of forever things that last eternally, and joy is foremost among them. The prophet Isaiah speaks of *everlasting joy* three times, and three is the ultimate number of witness. [*"Every matter must be established by the testimony of two or three witnesses"* (2 Corinthians 13:1*b*, NIV)]. It is well established, therefore, that joy is everlasting!

How could joy be less than perpetual when the sources for our joy are eternal? We have viewed God, the Bible, God's kingdom, and the divine Presence as primary sources of our joy, and all of these have their beginning and ending in eternity.

Joy and Our Walk with God

Paul and Gretel Haglin, long-term friends of mine and fellow ministers of the gospel of grace, recently wrote: "JOY is the barometer of our walk in the kingdom of God because JOY is the first to show and JOY is the first to go. When JOY is lost, it can be swiftly followed by the loss of peace, which then, believe it or not, actually exposes our righteousness to attack because we are in the process of losing our faith!"[1] We, then, cannot merely be exposed to the joy of God's kingdom. A steady, deep, and abiding joy requires that we daily walk and live in it. This joy is as perpetual as our walk in God's kingdom.

Since the source of our joy is eternal, the very nature of joy has to be unceasing. As long as the pump keeps working in the fountain, the plumes of water continue to rise skyward. In life, as long as God's divine presence is "pumping" in our lives, joy will spring up perpetually. Twice the prophet said, *"The ransomed of the LORD will return. They will enter Zion with singing; everlasting joy will crown their heads. Gladness and joy will over-*

take them, and sorrow and sighing will flee away" (Isaiah 35:10; 51:11, NIV). If, as many commentators say, the spiritual meaning of "Zion" is the Church, then the promise is for everlasting joy, expressed in gladness and singing, to be the environment of God's Church. When God's presence is among His people, eternal joy flows like a fountain. David expressed it this way: *"Thou wilt show me the path of life: in thy presence is fulness of joy; at thy right hand there are pleasures for evermore"* (Psalm 16:11, emphasis added). If our joy seems to have disappeared, it is likely that we are no longer close to God's right hand, for the pleasures there are *"for evermore."*

Some years ago when I was ministering in Australia, I picked up a copy of the Australian edition of the *Reader's Digest* and read a short item that gripped me. An Aussie visiting in America ran short of funds and found a temporary job taking a traffic survey in one of our major cities. He was seated on a stool at an intersection directly across from one of our major churches. He reported that Americans seem to go to church as a family unit. As they get out of their parked car, the father takes his son's hand while the mother holds the hand of their daughter and they joyfully, and even playfully, head for the church. However, as soon as they reach church property, all merriment ceases, and they walk into the building very solemnly.

At the end of the service, he observed that people paraded out of the building as though walking behind a casket at a funeral, but when their feet touched the curb away from the church, their behavior changed. The father loosened his tie and ruffled the boy's hair, while the mother and the daughter became playful again.

The writer asks the penetrating question, "What happens in American churches that so destroys the joy of living?"

What does happen to our joy if Zion (the Church) is to be a place of everlasting joy? Didn't Jesus promise the disciples, and us, *"You have sorrow now, but I will see you again and then you will rejoice; and no one can rob you of that joy"* (John 16:22, TLB)? Is it possible that many believers no longer see Jesus when they assemble to worship Him?

In the Haglin's newsletter, Paul and Gretel write:

Hear that! *"No one can rob you of that JOY!"*

But there are forces in this world of Satan's realm that delight in trying to rob us of our JOY, so that we might be so weak that they can waltz in and carry us and our household off into doubt and despair and depression—all the antithesis of JOY.

Satan's minions are sneaky! Some of these thieves shake us through other people's actions, others shake us with circumstances, while still others work quietly within us using our own thoughts to distract us from keeping our eyes on our Lord Jesus, in whose presence is fullness of JOY.

What we have to remember is Jesus' promise to us as His disciples that no one can take our JOY from us—unless we allow them to!—unless we deliberately give it to them by giving in to their temptations to doubt and embrace a "poor me" spirit!

When people are used to rob others of their JOY, the world calls them "kill-Joys" or "wet-blankets." We call them JOY ROBBERS!

They really are Satan's helpers, usually unwittingly to be sure, but Satan's helpers nevertheless; and for that moment, Satan's instruments. Remember poor Peter being sucked into being Satan's mouthpiece in Mark 8:33?

We need to learn how to avoid inadvertently being a JOY ROBBER ourselves, and how to stand against the ones that Satan wants to use on us!

Our JOY wants to flee under oppression like a heavy-handed boss, a nagging mother, a domineering husband, a dictatorial minister, a tyrannical head of state, or religious persecution. But in situations like these, we must hold steady on God's course and lift our faces toward heaven and rejoice, remembering Jesus' words, *"No one takes your JOY away from you!"* Not even death![2]

If, as Jesus promised, no one takes our joy from us, the loss of God's everlasting joy must come by our personal surrender of that joy. That joy came as a gift and we can surrender, ignore, or exchange it, but in doing so, we have no one to blame but ourselves.

Perpetuity is, indeed, a characteristic of joy. It is a gift from God that should remain in our lives throughout eternity, unlike temporary pleasure. Joy is not rooted in possessions, positions, popularity, or politics. Its roots are in the eternal God, His Word, His Spirit, and His kingdom, and these are eternal and unchangeable.

After all, joy is not an ice cream cone that will melt if not eaten. Joy is more like an apple tree that revives year after fruitful year. Although others may strip the tree of all its apples, they will grow back in another season, for the life of the tree is not in the apples. The fruit is merely a manifestation of that life. Similarly, people may strip us of our evidences of joy, but the true joy flows from the roots to the leaves. It is unaffected and it will again make itself known.

Joy remains long after pleasure has died. Joy outlives excitement and amusement. Joy is a force surpassing all other human emotions except love, and it can be communicated. Praise the Lord!

For Reflection
1. We know that at our conversion we receive everlasting life. Do we receive anything else that is everlasting?
2. What is a "kill-joy"? Have you unintentionally been a kill-joy in your relationships with others?
3. Contrast joy with pleasure; with excitement; with amusement.

Endnotes
1. Paul and Gretel Haglin, *Letters of Faith*, Resurrection Christian Ministries, Hawk Point, MO.
2. Ibid.

10

Joy Is Communicable

"Her neighbors and relatives heard that the Lord had shown her great mercy, and they shared her joy" (Luke 1:58, NIV).

We use the word *communicable* two different ways in our daily speech. First, we use it to describe the passing of a concept to another by spoken words, printed pages, gestures, or pictures, much as I am doing in the writing of this book. My thoughts are being communicated through printed words. The second meaning of the word *communicable* refers to something that can be transmitted from one to another. Joy fits both of these concepts.

That the concept of joy can be communicated is the theme of the third section of this book. The favorite Bible word for this act of expressing joy is *rejoice*. It occurs about 200 times in 187 separate verses in our Bible. It was unquestionably Paul's favorite praise word: he used it nearly 30 times in his brief epistles. We hear him say, *"Rejoice in the Lord always. I will say it again: Rejoice!"* (Philippians 4:4, NIV). Paul didn't want the believers to be joyful inwardly without also expressing it outwardly. Perhaps he was saying, "Let your face know what your heart feels."

As we'll see later, *rejoice* is an action, a command, a response, and a release. It is expressed verbally, physically, emotionally, and deliberately. We rejoice over God, and God rejoices over us. It is a beautiful word that combines love and joy in a common expression, for joy is ever dependent upon love. Perhaps that is why "love" is mentioned as the first fruit of the Spirit followed immediately by "joy."

In this chapter, however, I want to emphasize that the second meaning of the word *communicable* is a characteristic of joy. Much as AIDS is a communicable disease, joy is a communicable *blessing*. You can impart joy to others, infecting them, and you can also "catch" joy from joyful persons. It often comes as a simple by-product of a relationship with a person who has joy—especially Jesus.

Go to Him Outside the Camp

In the Old Testament, God decreed that persons with infectious leprosy be segregated from the camp, and that when they were approached by a non-leprous person, they must cry out from a distance, "Unclean, unclean!" This segregation was simply a way of preventing an infection of the entire camp with leprosy. Today, when we do this with a contagious disease, we call this action a "quarantine."

Expositors of the Bible have long used leprosy as an analogy to sin. Keeping this in mind, we can see that Jesus, who became our sin bearer at Calvary, had to be thrust out of the camp. He took our place in disgraceful exile—a leper. The book of Hebrews points out that Jesus was sacrificed for us outside the camp—was quarantined—and then suggests, *"Let us, then, go to him outside the camp, bearing the disgrace he bore"* (Hebrews 13:13, NIV). From God's point of view, Jesus died as an outcast, being isolated as a spiritual leper.

I don't think this was the view of the religious leaders who demanded the death of Jesus. They didn't view Him as a sin bearer. They didn't even accept Him as the Son of God. They saw Him as a troublemaker and a threat to their religious control of the people. Jesus just didn't fit the religious pattern of His day. He kept introducing something that religion has always had trouble with—JOY. How can you control a joyful people? Joy has set them free!

One of the disgraces Jesus carried with Him was being joyful in religious circumstances. For instance, *"On the last and greatest day of the Feast, Jesus stood and said in a loud voice, 'If a man is thirsty, let him come to me and drink. Whoever believes in me, as the Scripture has said, streams of living water will flow from within him'"* (John 7:37-38, NIV). In the midst of a most solemn religious ritual, Jesus offered the joy of the Spirit. He actually infected these saddened people with joy. Little wonder the Scribes, Pharisees, and High Priest wanted Jesus outside the camp. He was dangerous to their "religion," and therefore it was convenient to regard Him as expendable.

Jesus and His joy are still dangerous to religion, and those who have been infected with His joy are just as alarming. It is to be expected, then, that believers are thrust *"without the camp."* Our nearly sadistic society with its news emphasis on murders, shootings, drug deals, deceit, and dishonesty in high places doesn't know what to do with joyful persons. If they can't lock them up, they shut them out.

Seeing Jesus, We Are Filled with Joy

Jesus infected people with joy during His entire lifetime. In fact, just seeing Jesus induced joy. After the shepherds saw Christ in the manger, *"The shepherds returned, glorifying and praising God for all the things they had heard and seen, which were just as they had been told"* (Luke 2:20, NIV). They saw Jesus and they were filled with joy.

Matthew's account of Christ's birth tells of the coming of the wise men. After consulting with King Herod, they again saw the star that had guided them to Jerusalem. Matthew says, *"When they saw the star, they rejoiced with exceeding great joy"* (Matthew 2:10).

The cripples who could now walk, the blind who could now see, the demonized who were set free, and the sick who were healed all went home filled with joy, and their joy infected others. This continued during the ministry of the apostles. When Philip preached Christ in the city of Samaria, *"With shrieks, evil spirits came out of many, and many paralytics and cripples were healed. So there was great joy in that city"* (Acts 8:7,8, NIV). The preaching of Christ with signs and wonders following still imparts a glorious joy to both the participants and the observers.

After the trauma of the crucifixion, the disciples hid themselves in the Upper Room. When Jesus rose from the dead, He paid them a visit and explained the purpose of the cross. *"After he said this, he showed them his hands and side. The disciples were overjoyed when they saw the Lord"* (John 20:20, NIV). Consistently throughout the Bible, those who saw Jesus were filled with joy. This still happens today!

Sight is a great joy inducer. It often communicates joy faster than words. We live in a visual society that seems to learn more through the eye gate than through the ear gate. This affects the whole person. Merely hearing spiritual truths is probably insufficient for today's generation. We need to see. The cry of the Greeks who came to Philip, *"Sir, we would see Jesus"* (John 12:21), needs to become our daily cry, for when our spiritual eyes are opened to see Jesus, His glorious love and joy fill our inner beings.

Catch His Joy

While sight is the most dominant joy inducer, association with joyful persons will also infect us with joy. It is difficult to be around a person bubbling with joy without being infused with joy ourselves. People in a depressed state seldom want to be around joyful persons, for joy conflicts with their inner feelings; however, if they will permit the association, it probably will lift them out of their depression.

When Titus brought back a good report from the Corinthian church, Paul reported, *"Therefore we were comforted in your comfort: yea, and exceedingly the more joyed we for the joy of Titus, because his spirit was refreshed by you all"* (2 Corinthians 7:13). The joy in Corinth infected Titus, and this joy soon became joy in Paul.

The adage is old, but the truth is eternal: "If you want to be happy, surround yourself with happy people." The principle well adapts to joy. If you want to live a joyful life, associate with joyful persons. They will infect you with their joy.

Sometimes it doesn't take more than a testimony to impart joy from one to another. When Paul and Barnabas went to Jerusalem to report to the apostles, *"...they passed through Phenice and Samaria, declaring the conversion of the Gentiles: and they caused great joy unto all the brethren"* (Acts 15:3). Their joyful testimony of what God was doing among the Gentiles infused the believers with increased joy.

I was raised in a religious culture that regularly had "testimony services" where believers shared what God was doing in their lives. I remember how some of those testimonies lifted our spirits and produced an atmosphere of rejoicing in the listeners. Today's hurried worship schedules do not seem to allow for testimonies anymore, but in cutting them out, we've lost one source of the flow of joy.

It is always great to hear what God is doing in the lives of others. The reports of revival and renewal in other areas stir a fresh joy in our hearts as well as a longing to have some of those fires burning locally.

When Paul was a prisoner in Rome, he wrote a letter to the believers in Philippi saying, *"If you have any encouragement from being united with Christ, if any comfort from his love, if any fellowship with the Spirit, if any tenderness and compassion, then make my joy complete by being like-minded, having the same love, being one in spirit and purpose"* (Philippians 2:1-2, NIV). There was little in the way of natural circumstances to make Paul joyful. Roman prison was very crude, but he felt his joy would be made complete by hearing that the believers in Phillipi were walking in love. They would be an encouragement to the great apostle, and he could vicariously share in their joy.

In our busy world, we often overlook how a card or letter may be the encouragement and joy another believer needs. During the two years I was being treated for cancer, Essie Jackson from Silver Spring, Maryland, sent me a card at least monthly sharing a brief message of encouragement and love. Although my cancer is now in declared remission and I am again traveling in ministry, Sister Jackson still sends me an occasional card. What a joy producer this has been! She has never written a book nor, to my knowledge, preached a sermon, but she has shared her joy in the Lord by helping me to identify with her joy in Jesus.

Sustained by Another's Joy

Another glorious characteristic of joy is that it will flow from identification. When we are pressed beyond measure and our joy seems to have dissipated, we can often identify with the joy of another. This is often true in a marriage. It is wonderful when one partner is joy-filled at the time that the other partner is full of gloom. It can balance the atmosphere in the home and lift the spirit of the saddened one. This sharing of joy is probably the reason Jesus sent His disciples out in pairs, and why this is the preferred way of ministry. We can share strengths, courage, and joy.

Paul asked, *"How can we thank God enough for you in return for all the joy we have in the presence of our God because of you?"* (1 Thessalonians 3:9, NIV). This apostle had watched these believers step from darkness into light, and from being heathens to being new creations in Christ. Their joy was so infectious that even remembering them years later brought joy to this aging preacher of the Gospel of Christ. Paul's long-term identification with these believers reactivated his joy in Jesus. It is wise to keep in touch with those who have a joy in the Lord, especially if we were instrumental in inducing joy in them in the first place.

The obverse side of this coin is equally true. While Paul shared in the joy of the Thessalonian believers, he was relieved that the Corinthian believers, whom he had so severely rebuked, were now sharing in his joy. He wrote, *"I had confidence in all of you, that you would all share my joy"* (2 Corinthians 2:3*b*, NIV). He had earlier told them, *"...we work with you for your joy..."* (2 Corinthians 1:24, NIV). Paul felt that sharing joy was a give-and-take proposition. So should we. Take joy from a believer when you lack joy, and share joy with other believers when you abound in God's joy. This way we can "share the wealth."

Do you feel this is beyond you? Do you think that only persons of a certain personality can live joy-filled lives? Think again! JOY is a choice!

For Reflection

1. If joy is a noun, what is its verb form? Is it an active or passive verb? Why did Paul use it so much?
2. Can joy be infectious? Should it be? Are you a carrier?
3. Jesus was a dangerous carrier of joy. List four times you can think of that Jesus infected others with joy. Has He infected you lately?

11

Joy Is a Choice

"…they rested and made it a day of feasting and joy" (Esther 9:18, NIV).

This chapter title is accurate both from God's perspective and from our experience. Joy exists because God chose to make this blessing available to us. The same God who said, *"Let there be light: and there was light"* (Genesis 1:3), spoke joy into existence. God willed that there be joy. He designated joy as one of three foundations to His kingdom (*"righteousness and peace and joy in the Holy Spirit,"* Romans 14:17, NKJ), and He listed joy as the second fruit of the Spirit to ripen in a believer's life. Both in heaven and on earth, God's joy reigns.

We who access this joy do not create the joy—God is the creator of everything. By God's provision, joy is as available as air or water; but just as we must breathe the air or drink the water to benefit from them, possessing joy requires action on our part. It is a choice we must make.

From our perspective, we do not will joy into being. We *choose* to accept or reject the availability of joy. Joy is a present reality whether we access it or not. It may seem that I am viewing the world through rose-tinted glasses in insisting that joy is constantly available, but I am far too much of a realist to do that. In presenting the theology of joy and its characteristics of being a gift and a perpetual, communicable energy, I do not mean to suggest that an inner joy is a natural reflex for a believer. God's provision of joy is available at all times, but the appropriation of that joy requires an act of our will.

The great men of the Bible knew this. David sang, *"I will be glad and rejoice in thee: I will sing praise to thy name, O thou most High,"* and, *"That I may shew forth all thy praise in the gates of the daughter of Zion: I will rejoice in thy salvation"* (Psalm 9:2,14, emphasis added). David was not joyful because God exempted him from pressure, problems, and persecution. The Old Testament book of 1 Samuel supplies ample proof of the difficult, and sometimes tragic, circumstances in David's life. David was joyful because he had made a choice to joy in the Lord.

Similarly, Paul and Silas, who were illegally arrested, beaten, and thrown into a dungeon at Philippi, *"...at midnight... prayed, and sang praises unto God: and the prisoners heard them"* (Acts 16:25). This was not the response of happy emotions. These men would be masochists if they were happy under these circumstances. Their songs of praise came as a deliberate act of their wills. They chose to embrace the joy of the Lord in prayer and praise rather than commiserate with one another over their contemptible state. You remember the rest of the story. God sent an earthquake to accompany the singing, and the jailer not only released Paul and Silas, but also accepted Jesus as his Savior. Their choice of joy brought victory to all who were concerned.

Rev. Norman Vincent Peale, the great exponent of the power of positive thinking, once wrote this:

> The greatest power we have is the power of choice. It's an actual fact that if you've been moping in unhappiness, you can choose to be joyous instead and, by effort, lift yourself into joy. If you tend to be fearful, you can overcome that misery by choosing to have courage. Even in darkest grief you have a choice. The whole trend and quality of anyone's life is determined in the long run by the choices that are made.[1]

There are many choices in life that are made *for* us rather than *by* us. People don't choose their parents or childhood circumstances, but we can choose our own direction in life. We can choose our attitudes in life, and we can choose to embrace God's proffered joy in spite of life's circumstances.

Life is not inherently pleasant—it is a struggle.

> Pain in this life is inevitable—soul and body sufferings are a part of this life ever since our first ancestors broke God's word. We live in a sin-filled world and we are impacted by our own sin, but misery is optional! We are given freedom by God to be

as miserable as we want to be. Some people get more "mileage" out of being miserable than others because they thrive on the sympathy and the attention they receive![2]

Many years ago when I was pastor of a small, but growing, congregation in Kennewick, Washington, I was thrilled to have a visitor attend a Thursday evening prayer meeting. When the opportunity for spoken requests was given, she took up a large block of time telling us about her unsaved husband and the misery he caused in her life and in the home. We joined her in earnest prayer for his salvation for many months after this. Men in the congregation put legs to our prayers and looked up this man and invited him to church. Eventually he came and gave his heart to Jesus.

Expecting a response of great rejoicing from his wife, I was shocked to notice that she had stopped attending church. Now the husband was requesting prayer for his wife. Whereas she had been the object of our attention, now he got all the attention.

For several years we could not get this husband and wife to serve the Lord together. They took turns. Somehow it seemed that they enjoyed the attention they got by projecting their misery to the little flock of believers. It may have been subconscious, but they had made a deliberate choice to be miserable rather than joyful. In the grace of God, the two of them finally found joy in the Lord as a team before the husband died.

It is God's will that we walk in joy. His provision of joy is unbounded and totally unconnected with our circumstances in life. Oswald Chambers reminds us, "God regenerates us and puts us in contact with all his divine resources, but he cannot make us walk according to his will."[3]

Of all creation, only man can say yes or no to God. This means that regardless of circumstances, each man lives in a world of his own making. It can be filled with God's joy or it can be lived in misery and sorrow. Life does not make these choices for us; we do. Most of us have encountered persons who came from poverty, abuse, and rejection, but chose to live in the joy of the Lord. They sparkle against a dark background like a diamond under the jeweler's light.

Conversely, we've watched persons with education, security, and affluence choose to live very unhappy lives. They turned to drugs, alcohol, or some other form of escapism to survive. It was a choice they made.

"But," you say, "no one in his or her right mind would choose to be unhappy."

You may be right. They simply did not choose to be happy. Harry Emerson Fosdick said, "It is this way. The Lord, he is always voting for a man; and the devil, he is always voting against him. Then the man himself votes and that breaks the tie."[4] How sad that so many believers vote with the devil and consign themselves to a joyless existence, when a simple vote with the Lord would have brought them into a bountiful life of joy. Perhaps Joshua's challenge to the elders of Israel is needed—*"...choose you this day whom ye will serve"* (Joshua 24:15a).

When Israel and Judah sat in Babylonian captivity, Isaiah foretold the coming of Jesus and His purpose. *"To appoint unto them that mourn in Zion, to give unto them beauty for ashes, the oil of joy for mourning, the garment of praise for the spirit of heaviness; that they might be called trees of righteousness, the planting of the LORD, that he might be glorified"* (Isaiah 61:3). This is the great divine exchange. To have God's beauty, we must turn in our ashes. To glow with the oil of joy, we must surrender our mourning, and God offers the garment of praise for the spirit of heaviness. To live in the joy of God, we must walk out of the gloom of life's situations. God does not make the oil of joy available to anoint our spirit of mourning—He asks that we trade in our pining so we can be anointed to praise. We must take off the spirit of heaviness to receive the garment of praise, for this garment is not an overcoat to be worn over a jacket of heaviness.

Isaiah was illustrating what Oswald Chambers much later said: "Will is the whole man active. I cannot *give up* my will; I must exercise it. I must *will* to obey, and I must *will* to receive God's Spirit [of joy]."[5] We cannot passively surrender our will to God; we must actively do what He asks us to do if we would live in divine joy rather than human misery.

When there are no negative circumstances troubling our lives, we find it easy and convenient to walk in joy, but life itself teaches us that the world, the flesh, and the devil are constantly tempting us out of our joy into the muck of sinful struggle. James wrote a solution to this problem, *"My brethren, count it all joy when ye fall into divers temptations"* (James 1:2).

Weymouth translates it, *"...reckon it nothing but joy..."* while Knox says, *"...consider yourselves happy..."*

Notice they used accountant terms. It suggests that we put these temptations to the credit side of the ledger rather than on the debit side. We can make an asset out of an apparent liability by an act of our will. We don't have to submit to any temptation to abandon joy. Instead we can use the temptation as a goad or reminder to deliberately walk in joy. It is all a matter of mind-set, but the sooner we make up our mind to live in joy, the better off we will be, for "If you don't make up your mind, your unmade mind will unmake you."[6]

"There is, however, a price-tag for us to pay for walking in JOY. The coins of the kingdom required to pay this price are unqualified love, forgiveness, perseverance, faithfulness, and endurance, and sometimes even sorrow. But remember what God promises us, *"...I will turn [your] mourning into JOY, and will comfort [you], and give [you] JOY for [your] sorrow"* (Jeremiah 31:13).[7]

The apostle James tells us that walking in joy is far more than mind over matter. It goes beyond positive thinking. He says that it is as much a matter of turning to God as it is a turning from joy killers. He writes, *"Come near to God and he will come near to you. Wash your hands, you sinners, and purify your hearts, you double-minded. Grieve, mourn and wail. Change your laughter to mourning and your joy to gloom"* (James 4:8-9, NIV). The upward look will always counterbalance the outward or inward look.

The minor prophet, Habakkuk, paints this picture beautifully. In chapter one, he reviews the devastation invading armies are inflicting, and he charges God with great unfairness. Then he retreats to his watchtower to seek the face of God in prayer. After meeting God and regaining the upward view, he concludes his book with, *"Though the fig tree does not bud and there are no grapes on the vines, though the olive crop fails and the fields produce no food, though there are no sheep in the pen and no cattle in the stalls, yet I will rejoice in the LORD, I will be joyful in God my Savior"* (Habakkuk 3:17-18, NIV).

He paints the bleakest possible picture of a scorched earth policy of invasion and the famine it induces, but his eyes are so fixed on God that he says, *"Though...yet I will rejoice in the Lord."* Even though at times there is little to nothing left in our lives over which to rejoice, God is ever present and is always unchanged by our circumstances. When life deals us an extreme negative season, we need to join this prophet in declaring our own *"Though...yet I will rejoice in the Lord."*

In speaking of *love*, the first fruit of the Spirit, Paul taught that nothing in this life could separate us from it. Would that not equally hold true of the second fruit of the Spirit, *joy*— especially when love, joy, and peace form the first cluster of the Spirit's fruit? Paul wrote:

> *Who shall separate us from the love* [or JOY] *of Christ? Shall trouble or hardship or persecution or famine or nakedness or danger or sword? As it is written: "For your sake we face death all day long; we are considered as sheep to be slaughtered." No, in all these things we are more than conquerors through him who loved us. For I am convinced that neither death nor life, neither angels nor demons, neither the present nor the future, nor any powers, neither height nor depth, nor anything else in all creation, will be able to separate us from the love* [or JOY] *of God that is in Christ Jesus our Lord* (Romans 8:35-39, NIV).

Any astute reader will see that Paul has covered almost anything in life, death, the world of mankind, and the spirit world. NOTHING can separate us from God's love, joy, and peace <u>except</u> us. These are eternal qualities, but we are eternal beings with authority over our attitudes, emotions, and wills. We can will to be sorrowful, bitter, revengeful, or we can choose to live in the love and joy of the Holy Spirit.

We may not always have the same level of joy, for joy is measurable, but we never need to be completely without joy.

For Reflection

1. If inner joy is not a natural reflex for a believer, how does he or she come into joy?
2. If, as I say, "Each man lives in a world of his own making," whose fault is it if you live a joyless life?

3. There is a price tag for walking in joy. List four or more coins of the kingdom required to pay this price. Is joy worth this price to you?

Endnotes

1. Norman Vincent Peale, as quoted in the February 1999 issue of *Bits and Pieces*, Copyright © 1999, The Economics Press, Inc., Caldwell, NJ.
2. Paul and Gretel Haglin's, *Letters of Faith,* Resurrection Christian Ministries, Hawk Point, MO.
3. Oswald Chambers, Entry 1143—*Draper's Book of Quotations for the Christian World*, Edythe Draper, Copyright © 1992, Tyndale House Publishers, Inc., Wheaton, IL.
4. Ibid., Harry Emerson Fosdick, Entry 1146.
5. Oswald Chambers, *My Utmost for His Highest*, pg. 138, Copyright © 1963 by Discovery House Publishers, Grand Rapids, MI.
6. Paul and Gretel Haglin's, *Letters of Faith*, Resurrection Christian Ministries, Hawk Point, MO.
7. E. Stanley Jones, *Leadership*, Vol. 17, No 2.

12

Joy Is Measurable

"...And their joy was very great" (Nehemiah 8:17, NIV).

There are different intensities of sunlight, but only one sun. When we have clear skies, the sun shines in all its brilliance; but when the clouds roll in, the sun's light is diffused and filtered. Differences in cloud intensities determine the amount of sunlight that comes through, but it will always come through. There are no clouds that can turn day into night. That's why the darkness at the crucifixion of Jesus was such a sign and wonder to the observers.

Similarly, we experience different intensities of joy during our lifetime. We experience and love cloudless times of life when pure joy radiates into us—unfiltered and unrestricted. Yet we don't have to live too many years to realize that this utopia is not forever. Clouds will form between us and the joy of the Lord. How wonderful to know that in spite of clouds of grief, pain, sorrow, and disappointment, joy is always shining above us.

It is unfair to take the simplistic view that says we either have joy or we do not. Joy, like so many other things in life, is not black or white, present or absent. There are intermediate shades of gray. There are degrees of joy. Joy is measurable.

Jesus said, *"Give, and it will be given to you. A good measure, pressed down, shaken together and running over, will be poured into your lap. For with the measure you use, it will be measured to you"* (Luke 6:38, NIV). God gives to us as we, in obedience, give to Him. We set the measure of God's gifts to us. Is it possible that we ourselves set the measure of God's joy we receive by the way we pour out the joy He has already given?

Similarly, Paul taught that God's *faith* comes by measure. He wrote, *"For by the grace given me I say to every one of you: Do not think of yourself more highly than you ought, but rather think of yourself with sober judgment, in accordance with the measure of faith God has given you"* (Romans 12:3, NIV). Every believer is blessed with a measure of faith, or it would have been impossible to get saved, *"For by grace are ye saved <u>through faith</u>; and that not of yourselves: it is the gift of God"* (Ephesians 2:8, emphasis added). Faith for salvation, however, is but a beginning measure of faith. When faith is used, it can grow, mature, and multiply mightily in our lives.

Even God's grace comes by measure, for the Bible says, *"But unto every one of us is given grace according to the measure of the gift of Christ"* (Ephesians 4:7).

If God's gifts, faith, and grace are measurable and can increase through use and a closer relationship with Jesus, shouldn't we expect that divine joy may have small beginnings and yet increase more and more in intensity and manifestation? How can we access great joy for our entire lives?

Since joy has its origins in the triune God, the more intimate and consistent our relationship with God, the greater measure of joy we will possess. Some persons barely bubble with joy while others cascade high into the air in God's fountain of joy.

When I sat in the lobby of the hotel in Forth Worth, Texas, and watched the fountain send forth cascades of water, I recognized different heights and intensities in the crests. Although there was no complete uniformity, there was still absolute beauty. There are times when joy forces our emotions into extreme highs while at other times, the expression of that joy is much lower—but it is all joy produced by the divine pump deep in our souls. Whatever level of joy may be bubbling in our souls, it is beautiful; but it can probably be increased in its intensity, thereby increasing its beauty.

I see five levels of joy mentioned in the Bible. Since five is the number of grace, each level contributes to a higher manifestation of the grace of God in the believer's life.

First, there is the <u>contrast</u> Jesus spoke of between <u>your joy and My joy</u>. Jesus told His disciples, *"These things have I spoken unto you, that my joy might remain in you, and that your joy might be full"* (John 15:11). Far too many persons fear that if they give their lives to the Lord, they will lose their joy in living. Jesus taught the exact opposite. He offers us double joy—His joy *and* our joy. He does not ask that we give up our natural joy. He suggests that He wants *our* joy to be full, but Christ also wants to have *His* joy flowing in our lives—giving the believer the best of both worlds, heaven and earth.

The second measurement of joy the Bible speaks of is full joy. Peter mentioned this on the day of Pentecost. While he was preaching Jesus to the crowd, he used the psalmist's quote of Jesus, *"You have made known to me the paths of life; you will fill me with joy in your presence"* (Acts 2:28, NIV, emphasis added). Jesus expected to be filled with God's joy. So can we.

The Apostle John felt that being filled with joy was available to believers. He wrote, *"These things write we unto you, that your joy may be full"* (1 John 1:4, emphasis added). Furthermore, in his next letter he said, *"Having many things to write unto you, I would not write with paper and ink: but I trust to come unto you, and speak face to face, that our joy may be full"* (2 John 1:12, emphasis added).

Paul also expected to be filled with joy, for he told Timothy, *"...I long to see you, so that I may be filled with joy"* (2 Timothy 1:4, NIV). Interestingly enough, the source of this fullness of joy would come out of Christian relationship. When believers relate lovingly, their mingled joy increases in each of them.

Every fiber of our being can vibrate with the joy of the Lord. We are such small creatures when compared with God that it doesn't take much of His joy to fill us. A thimbleful will do, but we definitely need that small measure of joy in our spirits.

A third measurement of joy is exceeding joy. Whatever being "filled with joy" may constitute, there is a level of joy that far exceeds it. The psalmist is the first to speak of this level of joy. He wrote, *"Let the righteous be glad; let them rejoice before God: yea, let them exceedingly rejoice"* (Psalm 68:3). He uses the verb form of joy, *rejoice*, but he wants the righteous to *"exceedingly rejoice."* This would be the release of a level of joy beyond *your joy*, *my joy*, and *full joy*. It is all that plus more. It is a joy that exceeds anything yet experienced.

When we were first saved, we received Christ's joy. When the Holy

Spirit took up His residence in us, we certainly experienced full joy, but the glorious mystery is that there is even more joy available to the believer who will press in closer to Jesus.

Peter connected this level of joy with the revelation of Christ's glory when he wrote, *"But rejoice, inasmuch as ye are partakers of Christ's sufferings; that, when his glory shall be revealed, ye may be glad also with exceeding joy"* (1 Peter 4:13). Some persons put this entirely into the future, but Peter did not say exceeding joy would come when Jesus returned, but when *"his glory shall be revealed."* If the glory is the manifest presence of God, then a measure of that glory is now available to the Church, since God is demonstrating His presence in many different ways in many various places. Surely this is a generation that can enter into God's *"exceeding joy."*

Perhaps some of the joylessness of modern Christians can be traced to what they are seeking. Some want signs, wonders, prophecies, and miracles while others want visitations of angels and visions, but these do not bring *"exceeding joy."* It is the presence of Jesus that lifts us to this higher level of joy. Concerning this experience, David wrote, *"You have made known to me the path of life; you will fill me with joy in your presence, with eternal pleasures at your right hand"* (Psalm 16:11, NIV). There is obviously joy in what Christ has done for us, but there is a far higher level of joy in His presence.

Jude seemed to see this, for he concluded his brief book with, *"And he is able to keep you from slipping and falling away, and to bring you, sinless and perfect, into his glorious presence with mighty shouts of everlasting joy. Amen"* (Jude 1:25, TLB). This may be God's ultimate plan, but I believe it is being accomplished progressively, step by step, in our here and now. We are now being brought into His presence, and this is inducing an exceedingly great joy that produces "mighty shouts."

When telling of the great generosity of the Macedonian churches, Paul wrote, *"Out of the most severe trial, their overflowing joy and their extreme poverty welled up in rich generosity"* (2 Corinthians 8:2, NIV, emphasis added). This seems to be a fourth measurement of joy—overflowing joy. A person with this level of joy cannot contain it. It is bigger than he or she can handle—it simply overflows.

All of us love to be around a person experiencing "overflowing joy." It splashes over everyone who gets close. It is as infectious as boisterous laughter, and it brings healing everywhere it goes, for, *"A merry heart doeth good like a medicine"* (Proverbs 17:22a).

There is only one measurement of joy that is higher than "overflowing joy." It is "inexpressible joy." It was the fisherman Peter who said, *"Though you have not seen him, you love him; and even though you do not see him now, you believe in him and are filled with an inexpressible and glorious joy"* (1 Peter 1:8, NIV).

My dog illustrates this conundrum of being filled with joy greater than our ability to express it. When I return from a trip, he meets me at the front door wild with excitement. He wants me to pick him up so he can lick my face. Then he wants to get down so he can run circles in the house. He'll bring me one of his toys, then roll over and kick his feet in the air. He is so filled with joy and tries every way he knows to show it. Sometimes he exhausts himself in his effort to demonstrate his joy at having me home.

I can relate to that. There are times that being in the presence of Jesus so fills me with inexpressible joy that I try every form of expression I have successfully used in the past to release it. I sing, praise, shout, dance, laugh, and weep in such quick succession it appears that I am trying to do them all simultaneously. This all gives expression to the inner joy, but the joy is coming in far faster than I can get it out in rejoicing.

The King James Version translates this phrase as, *"joy unspeakable and full of glory."* It is a joy greater than words can express. It is so inexpressible that even body language cannot fully release it. It is involved with the glory of God—His manifest presence—and He generates joy faster than we can handle it. This must be the ultimate level of joy God can give to believers.

Yes, joy is measurable. It goes from "your joy" to "full joy" to "exceeding joy" to "overflowing joy" to the ultimate of "inexpressible joy." Please don't make the mistake of seeing these as different levels of the expressions of joy. These are actually different levels of joy. It is the same product, but different quantities. Some persons seem to have an ounce of joy, others a full pound, while still others press into God's presence and end up with a ton of joy.

Perhaps an ounce of joy is overwhelming to persons who have lived joyless lives before they met Jesus at Calvary, but there is more. The amount of joy that flows into us, and subsequently through us, will be determined by our relationship with the great joy producer—God! The closer we get to Him, the more of His glorious joy will be released to us. It is automatic, for God's joy is a byproduct of His glory, and His manifest presence is what we call His glory.

While the world spends billions of dollars for a cheap substitute for joy—entertainment and/or happiness—believers need do no more than regularly come into God's presence to be filled with "inexpressible joy."

A great southern Gospel song reminds us, "If the world didn't give it to you, the world can't take it away." Hallelujah! Our joy is secure in Christ Jesus.

My friends, the Haglins, remind us: "JOY is therefore worth guarding! And, if we guard our JOY, our JOY will guard us—guard our mind, and our heart, and our strength!

"JOY is a mind-set, not just a feeling!

"JOY is an attitude!

"JOY is a posture!

"JOY is a position!

"JOY requires commitment, courage, and the capacity to endure!

"JOY is a decision and a choice!

"JOY is a grace!

"Remember: an attitude of gratitude brings JOY!"[1]

Do we deserve this joy? Of course not. It comes as an extension of God's great mercy to us.

For Reflection

1. In what way would you say that joy is measurable?
2. The amount of joy that flows into us, and subsequently through us, will be determined by _____.
3. List five levels of joy seen in the New Testament.

Endnotes

1. Paul and Gretel Haglin, *Letters of Faith,* Resurrection Christian Ministries, Hawk Point, MO.

13

Joy Is a Response to Grace

"The Lord is my strength and my shield; my heart trusts in Him and I am helped. My heart leaps for joy and I will give thanks to Him in song" (Psalm 28:7, NIV).

In the preceding chapter, I pointed out that there are five levels of joy mentioned in the Bible. Since five is the number of grace, each level contributes to a higher manifestation of the grace of God in the believer's life.

Martin Luther reminded us that "Christ is no Moses, no exacter, no giver of laws, but a giver of grace, a Savior; he is infinite mercy and goodness, freely and bountifully given to us."[1] God is no faultfinder—always looking for things to condemn in us. He estimates us at our best, not our worst. The Bible tells us, *"...the LORD your God is gracious and merciful, and will not turn away his face from you, if ye return unto him"* (2 Chronicles 30:9*b*). This promise by itself is a joy producer in our lives.

What Is This Thing Called Grace?

Defining grace has always been difficult since grace is so unlimited. Its boundaries are the same as God's. Perhaps A.W. Tozer gave us as rounded a definition of grace as we're going to find:

Grace is the good pleasure of God that inclines him to bestow benefits upon the undeserving. It is a self-existent principle inherent in the divine nature and appears to us as a self-caused propensity to pity the wretched, spare the guilty, welcome the outcast, and bring into favor those who were before under just disapprobation. Its use to us sinful men is to save us and make us sit together in heavenly places to demonstrate to the ages the exceeding riches of God's kindness to us in Christ Jesus.[2]

Grace is far more than God's forgiveness, although forgiveness flows out of God's grace. "Grace is an energy; not a mere sentiment; not a mere thought of the Almighty; not even a word of the Almighty. It is as real an energy as the energy of electricity. It is a divine energy; it is the energy of the divine affection rolling in plenteousness toward the shores of human need."[3]

God purposes that we live in His grace and extend it to others. How quickly do persons who have been rescued by God's grace slip into a works righteousness that produces a false religious pride with dependence upon behavior rather than upon believing. This can happen more rapidly than you would believe possible.

For example, the last move of God known as the Charismatic move, has already descended into legalism in most places, and legalism is a great joy killer. Legalism is an internal set of rules, schedules, or expectations that we have learned and to which we feel we must adhere. Failure brings loss of joy and plunges us into frantic anxiety!

Paul had to address this problem of legalism in the Galatian church. He wrote the following:

> *You foolish Galatians! Who has bewitched you? Before your very eyes Jesus Christ was clearly portrayed as crucified. I would like to learn just one thing from you: Did you receive the Spirit by observing the law, or by believing what you heard? Are you so foolish? After beginning with the Spirit, are you now trying to attain your goal by human effort? Have you suffered so much for nothing—if it really was for nothing? Does God give you his Spirit and work miracles among you because you observe the law, or because you believe what you heard?* (Galatians 3:1-5, NIV).

Paul was exhorting the Galatian believers to remember that they were perfected by the grace of God, through the Holy Spirit, not by the works of the flesh, even though that is the desire of our carnal nature. It is only the Holy Spirit who releases the indescribable JOY within us! It is the Holy Spirit who will guard that indwelling joy if we will let Him!

Legalistic Expectations

We must continue to keep our human spirits free from any form of legalism to live in God's grace. We alone can do that for ourselves. Paul reminded these poor deceived believers, *"It is for freedom that Christ has set us free. Stand firm, then, and do not let yourselves be burdened again by a yoke of slavery"* (Galatians 5:1, NIV). We dare not exchange God's grace for our actions.

When we exchange our freedom in Christ for the rules and expectations of legalism, it often breeds a contempt for those who stumble or show some kind of weakness. We may take the position of "grace for me; law for you." Legalism leads to unholy comparisons. Either we begin to realize that we will never measure up to the standard of the Super Saint, and hence slide into self-condemnation and depression, or we delight in comparing our "spiritual report card" with struggling believers and discover that we are, indeed, being more holy than they—at least according to our list of holy actions and saintly standards. Either way, we will lose our joy.

What a far cry this is from the glorious liberty we once enjoyed in worshiping Jesus. We are the losers; but Jesus loses too, for we become so self-centered that we cease being Christ-centered. "When the mask of self-righteousness has been torn from us and we stand stripped of all our accustomed defenses, we are candidates for God's generous grace."[4]

Once again, God's grace is coming to His people. This is the beginning of a new day. We are more than entering a new millennium of time—the winds of change are already blowing in the Church. Our "winter season" is about over; spring is near. Old methods and old leadership are giving place to new. We desperately need the joy of the Lord to enable us to accept and participate in this change, for change is distressing to most persons. Without the joy of the Lord, we may well return to religious politics and legalism, and end up with divisions and factions. We are never united by structure alone; we need the joy of the Lord that is found in the presence and the glory of the Lord.

The winds of revival that are blowing across our nation are bringing us new songs, new leadership, new spiritual manifestations, and renewed spiritual emphases. This has proven to be both threatening to the joy of some and a producer of joy in others. Those of us who were so active in an earlier move of God need a great measure of His grace to embrace what God is doing today, for it is very unlike what He did before. We must allow God to be God and to function as God rather than try to force Him to do now as He did in earlier days.

Perhaps it would help us to remember that the law didn't make anyone perfect. Why would we think that our laws of legalism could do what God's law didn't accomplish? True redemption does not come through observance of rules. The New Testament teaches us, *"For it is by grace you have been saved, through faith—and this not from yourselves, it is the gift of God—not by works, so that no one can boast"* (Ephesians 2:8-9, NIV). Paul repeats this when writing to Titus: *"Not by works of righteousness which we have done, but according to his mercy he saved us, by the washing of regeneration, and renewing of the Holy Ghost"* (Titus 3:5).

The great evangelist of an earlier age, Dwight Moody, said, "Law tells me how crooked I am; grace comes along and straightens me out."[5] Our only hope before our salvation was God's amazing grace. This remains our only hope subsequent to that salvation. We are no more capable of keeping ourselves saved than we were able to save ourselves. Our entire walk in God is because of His grace. What tension this releases; what joy this brings. His grace keeps me!

Why do we call grace amazing? Grace is amazing because it works against the grain of common sense. Hard-nosed common sense will tell you that you are too wrong to meet the standards of a holy God; pardoning grace tells you that it's all right in spite of so much in you that is wrong.

Realistic common sense tells you that you are too weak, too harassed, too human to change for the better; grace gives you power to send you on the way to being a better person. Plain common sense may tell you that you are caught in a rut of fate or futility; grace promises that you can trust God to have a better tomorrow for you than the day you have made for yourself.[6]

Saved to the Uttermost

What a basis for joy! Our past has been forgiven, our present is a vast improvement, and our future is secure in Christ. Grace saved us, is saving us, and shall save us to the uttermost.

When David realized this he sang, *"Let them shout for joy, and be glad, that favour my righteous cause: yea, let them say continually, Let the LORD be magnified, which hath pleasure in the prosperity of his servant"* (Psalm 35:27). We, too, should shout for joy while reveling in the grace of God.

Our salvation is a great joy producer. Remission from guilt, right standing with God, and entrance into God's wonderful family of believers bring a joy never before experienced. Even heaven rejoices when a sinner repents and is saved, and all this is an action and provision of God's great grace. In mercy, we are forgiven our sin-debt. In grace, we are given the life of God and all the benefits of sonship. What grace! What mercy! What a combination! What JOY!

John Bunyan wrote, "Grace can pardon our ungodliness and justify us with Christ's righteousness; it can put the Spirit of Jesus Christ within us; it can help us when we are down; it can heal us when we are wounded; it can multiply pardons, as we through frailty multiply transgressions."[7]

For believers, the most wonderful thing of all is not that our sins have been forgiven, nor that we may enjoy certain experiences and blessings as a Christian. The thing that should astound us is that we are children of God, part of God's people—God's family.

There will be no joy without God's grace, for there is no true joy outside the ranks of the redeemed. God's grace is the beginning of our gladness. Before His grace appeared on the horizon of our lives, there was gloom, uncertainty, fear, and sorrow. We sought for escape in amusement, entertainment, distraction, and idolatry, but none of these brought joy to our lives.

Admittedly we enjoyed seasons of pleasure, but not true joy. Of Moses it is said, *"He chose to be mistreated along with the people of God rather than to enjoy the pleasures of sin for a short time"* (Hebrews 11:25, NIV). Satan's selling point for sin is the pleasure it brings, but he never tells how fleeting those pleasures are. He also does not tell the participants how quickly he or she must move on to something wilder or more exciting to maintain the level of pleasure.

When God's grace comes into our lives, joy—true and eternal joy—comes to abide. This joy remains as long as we remain in the grace of God. Paul suggests, *"Let the word of Christ dwell in you richly in all wisdom; teaching and admonishing one another in psalms and hymns and spiritual songs, singing with grace in your hearts to the Lord"* (Colossians 3:16). He seemed to feel that grace in our hearts should be accompanied with joyful song.

The Marvelous Miracle of Grace

Sometimes we need a little reminder that we are what we are because of the grace of God. I recently read the following story that makes the point better than I could.

A large prosperous downtown church had three mission churches under its care that it had started. On the first Sunday of the New Year all the members of the mission churches came to the city church for a combined Communion service. In those mission churches, which were located in the slums of the city, were some outstanding cases of conversions—thieves, burglars, and so on—but all knelt side by side at the Communion rail. On one such occasion the pastor saw a former burglar kneeling beside a judge of the Supreme Court of England—the judge who had sent him to jail where he had served seven years. After his release this burglar had been converted and become a Christian worker. Yet, as they knelt there, the judge and the former convict, neither one seemed to be aware of the other.

After the service, the judge was walking home with the pastor and said to the pastor, "Did you notice who was kneeling beside me at the Communion rail this morning?"

The pastor replied, "Yes, but I didn't know that you noticed."

The two walked along in silence for a few more moments, and then the judge said, "What a miracle of grace."

The pastor nodded in agreement. "Yes, what a marvelous

miracle of grace."

Then the judge said, "But to whom do you refer?"

And the pastor said, "Why, to the conversion of that convict."

The judge said, "But I was not referring to him. I was thinking of myself."

The pastor, surprised, replied, "You were thinking of yourself? I don't understand."

"Yes," the judge replied, "it did not cost that burglar much to get converted when he came out of jail. He had nothing but a history of crime behind him, and when he saw Jesus as his Savior he knew there was salvation and hope and joy for him. And he knew how much he needed that help. But look at me. I was taught from earliest infancy to live as a gentleman; that my word was to be my bond; that I was to say my prayers, go to church, take Communion and so on. I went through Oxford, took my degrees, was called to the bar and eventually became a judge. Pastor, nothing but the grace of God could have caused me to admit that I was a sinner on a level with that burglar. It took much more grace to forgive me for all my pride and self-deception, to get me to admit that I was no better in the eyes of God than that convict that I had sent to prison."[8]

Quite frankly, we need not "sin that grace may abound." We are sinners and need only to confess that grace may abound. In that confession, we step into the amazing grace of our Lord Jesus Christ and become aware that His grace has brought us into His mercy.

For Reflection
1. How does embracing legalism destroy the joy in your life?
2. Why do we call grace "amazing"?
3. List four or more ways that grace and joy are interlinked.
4. Thank Him for that grace on a daily basis and His joy will fill your heart.

Endnotes

1. Martin Luther (1483-1546), Entry 5208—*Draper's Book of Quotations for the Christian World*, Edythe Draper, Copyright © 1992, Tyndale House Publishers, Inc., Wheaton, IL.

2. Ibid., A.W. Tozer (1897-1963), Entry 4652.

3. Ibid., Benjamin Jowett (1817-1893), Entry 5217.

4. Ibid., Erwin W. Lutzer (1941-), Entry 5238.

5. Ibid., D.L. Moody, *Christian History*, No. 25.

6. Lewis Smedes in *How Can It Be All Right When Everything Is All Wrong?* (quoted by Martin E. Marty in context). Christianity Today, Vol. 37, No. 8.

7. John Bunyan (1628-1688), Entry 5212—*Draper's Book of Quotations for the Christian World*, Edythe Draper, Copyright © 1992 by Tyndale House Publishers, Inc., Wheaton, IL.

8. James S. Hewett, *Illustrations Unlimited*, pg. 257, Copyright (C) 1988 by Tyndale House Publishers, Inc, Wheaton, IL.

14

Joy Is Released by Mercy

"Her neighbors and relatives heard that the Lord had shown her great mercy, and they shared her joy" (Luke 1:58, NIV).

It is difficult to discuss grace without also discussing mercy, for mercy is when we don't get what we deserve, while grace is when we get what we didn't deserve. Someone has suggested that mercy un-sins us, while grace positions us in Christ. We certainly need both. If grace is an occasion for joy, mercy must be at least equally so.

"Among the attributes of God, although they are all equal, mercy shines with even more brilliance than justice."[1] God has consistently revealed Himself to be a God of mercy. In fact, the word *mercy* is used 276 times in the King James Bible. Fifty-nine of those occurrences are in the New Testament.

When giving the law on Mount Sinai, God declared, *"...for I the LORD thy God am a jealous God, visiting the iniquity of the fathers upon the children unto the third and fourth generation of them that hate me; And shewing mercy unto thousands of them that love me, and keep my commandments"* (Exodus 20:5-6). A short season later in response to Moses' urgent plea for God to reveal Himself to him, we find this: *"And the LORD passed by before him, and proclaimed, The LORD, The LORD God, merciful and gracious, longsuffering, and abundant in goodness and truth. Keeping mercy for thousands, forgiving iniquity and transgression and sin, and that will by no means clear the guilty"* (Exodus 34:6-7a). God is merciful by nature. "God's wrath comes by measure; his mercy without measure."[2]

"I Will Sing of Mercy"

During the days of Christ's ministry on earth, a very common plea made to Him was, *"Have mercy on me."* Those who asked may have lacked a comprehension of grace, for they were living under a severe religious legal system; but they did understand mercy, and when they pled for it, Jesus extended it to them.

The psalmists had a grasp of the mercy of God, and they projected this mercy as an occasion for joyful responses to God. Hear them sing:

"I will sing of mercy and judgment: unto thee, O LORD, will I sing" (Psalm 101:1).

"O satisfy us early with thy mercy; that we may rejoice and be glad all our days" (Psalm 90:14).

"But I have trusted in thy mercy; my heart shall rejoice in thy salvation" (Psalm 13:5).

"But I will sing of thy power; yea, I will sing aloud of thy mercy in the morning: for thou hast been my defence and refuge in the day of my trouble" (Psalm 59:16).

These men who prophesied in song not only reveled in God's mercy, they encouraged us on repeated occasions, *"O give thanks unto the LORD; for he is good: because his mercy endureth for ever"* (Psalm 118:1). This assurance that God's *"mercy endureth for ever"* occurs in all twenty-six verses of Psalm 136. If mercy is everlasting, the joy that mercy produces should also be eternal.

The psalmists were not alone in coupling God's mercy with joy. The prophets also spoke of joy connected to God's mercy. Isaiah wrote, *"Sing, O heavens; and be joyful, O earth; and break forth into singing, O mountains: for the LORD hath comforted his people, and will have mercy upon his afflicted"* (Isaiah 49:13).

Jeremiah saw God's mercy and man's joy as connected. He said, *"The voice of joy, and the voice of gladness, the voice of the bridegroom, and the voice of the bride, the voice of them that shall say, Praise the LORD of hosts: for the LORD is good; for his mercy endureth for ever: and of them that shall bring the sacrifice of praise into the house of the LORD. For I will cause to return the captivity of the land, as at the first, saith the LORD"* (Jeremiah 33:11).

A Special Cause for Rejoicing

If anyone should be joyful and rejoice in God's grace and mercy, it should be us Gentiles. Paul, whom God made an apostle to the Gentiles, gives us special instruction:

> *Wherefore remember, that ye being in time past Gentiles in the flesh, who are called Uncircumcision by that which is called the Circumcision in the flesh made by hands; that at that time ye were without Christ, being aliens from the commonwealth of Israel, and strangers from the covenants of promise, having no hope, and without God in the world: But now in Christ Jesus ye who sometimes were far off are made nigh by the blood of Christ* (Ephesians 2:11-13).

Little wonder, then, that Paul declared that even the Gentiles sing for joy for God's mercy. He says, *"And that the Gentiles might glorify God for his mercy; as it is written, For this cause I will confess to thee among the Gentiles, and sing unto thy name"* (Romans 15:9).

But for the grace and mercy of God, we Gentiles would have no access to God, no right to His promises, and no provision for sin—*"But because of his great love for us, God, who is rich in mercy, made us alive with Christ even when we were dead in transgressions—it is by grace you have been saved"* (Ephesians 2:4-5, NIV). Remember, this was not written to the Hebrew believers; it was sent to the Gentiles in Ephesus.

What mercy and grace has been extended to us in not only offering us God's salvation, but in actually placing us into the chosen family of God. Five times in Romans 11, Paul speaks of us Gentiles having been grafted into God's olive tree. We are sharers in the same root structure God made available to His chosen people, the Jews. The same life flow that nourishes them also nourishes us. This means there is a constant source of heavenly joy flowing from the roots to the branches!

Approaching the Throne

As believers mature in their salvation, they come to know that there is no higher level of joy than when we are in God's presence. What mercy that we who were rebels are invited into the very presence of a sinless God. We asked for deliverance from hell, but we got admission to heaven!

We've discovered what David meant when he sang, *"Thou wilt show me the path of life: in thy presence is fulness of joy; at thy right hand there are pleasures for evermore"* (Psalm 16:11). God gives us many avenues of joy, but since He is ultimately the source of all our joys, the closer we get to the source, the greater the level of joy will be.

This principle is seen clearly in the book of Revelation. All through the book, we see increasing numbers of persons praising and worshiping God, but their highest release of joy was when they approached the throne of God. Isn't this true with us? As we sing, praise, and pray, we become aware of a special joy; but when we touch the presence of God, that level of joy enlarges, accelerates, and almost explodes within us. He is the cause of our rejoicing. He is the producer of our joy.

When offering us an acceptable route into God's presence, the psalmist wrote: *"Enter into his gates with thanksgiving, and into his courts with praise: be thankful unto him, and bless his name. For the LORD is good; his mercy is everlasting; and his truth endureth to all generations"* (Psalm 100:4-5). There is a way into God's presence because *"His mercy is everlasting."* Not only that, but we walk or run into God's presence through expressions of our joy in God. Joy in fact becomes the key. As we release whatever level of joy we have, we share in higher joys of God as we go through the gates into His presence.

Is any of this the result of our religious activity? Of course not. Is it the result of our spiritual knowledge? No! It is all because God's mercy has come to us, lifting us out of sin into His holy presence.

> *Praise be to the God and Father of our Lord Jesus Christ! In his great mercy he has given us new birth into a living hope through the resurrection of Jesus Christ from the dead, and into an inheritance that can never perish, spoil or fade—kept in heaven for you, who through faith are shielded by God's power until the coming of the salvation that is ready to be revealed in the last time. In this you greatly rejoice...* (1 Peter 1:3-6, NIV).

In considering mercy as a withholding of what we deserve, in contrast to grace—an extension from God of that which we do not deserve—we have to recognize that God has offered His joy as a reward to us. Both the Old Testament and the New Testament declare that God will reward us.

Through Isaiah, God promised, *"Behold, the Lord GOD will come with strong hand, and his arm shall rule for him: behold, his reward is with him, and his work before him"* (Isaiah 40:10). Jesus said, *"But thou, when thou prayest, enter into thy closet, and when thou hast shut thy door, pray to thy Father which is in secret; and thy Father which seeth in secret shall reward thee openly"* (Matthew 6:6).

In speaking of God's avenging of the righteous, we read, *"Then men will say, 'Surely the righteous still are rewarded; surely there is a God who judges the earth'"* (Psalm 58:11, NIV). King Solomon wrote: *"If thine enemy be hungry, give him bread to eat; and if he be thirsty, give him water to drink: For thou shalt heap coals of fire upon his head, and the LORD shall reward thee"* (Proverbs 25:21-22).

Martin Luther said, "Our office is a ministry of grace and salvation. It subjects us to great burdens and labors, dangers and temptations, with little reward or gratitude from the world. But Christ himself will be our reward if we labor faithfully."[3] Paul said, *"Whatever you do, work at it with all your heart, as working for the Lord, not for men, since you know that you will receive an inheritance from the Lord as a reward. It is the Lord Christ you are serving"* (Colossians 3:23,24, NIV).

Sharing His Reward

This promise of a reward is a divine motivation for us, but it is all an act of mercy. As we share God's mercy and grace with others, God shares His reward with us, but what is the nature of God's reward? Is it money in the bank or position in the eyes of others? No. His reward is far greater than this. Jesus told us what it would be in His story about the faithful steward, *"His lord said unto him, Well done, thou good and faithful servant: thou hast been faithful over a few things, I will make thee ruler over many things: enter thou into the joy of thy lord"* (Matthew 25:21).

God's highest reward for service faithfully done is, *"Enter into the joy of thy lord."* The New International Version translates this phrase as, *"Come and share your master's happiness!"* For that earthly servant it meant leaving the servants' quarters and moving into the main house. It was having food prepared for him rather than having to prepare the food for his master. It implies being promoted from the role of a servant to the position of a friend. It meant the best of everything in life, for he was invited to share in what made his master happy.

Didn't Jesus tell His disciples this? *"You are my friends if you do what I command. I no longer call you servants, because a servant does not know his master's business. Instead, I have called you friends, for everything that I learned from my Father I have made known to you"* (John 15:14-15, NIV). His reward to them for faithful service was movement from being servants to being friends.

So it is for us. We enter into the joy of our Lord as friends of God. What a phenomenal promise! God's reward is an invitation to share His happiness, to sit at His table with Him, and banquet with the King. No earthly "joy" can compare with this. This reward is the merciful privilege of living in God's presence and enjoying what God enjoys. It is God's ultimate reward.

So far we've seen the source of divine joy and a few of its characteristics. The third section of this book will be concerned with the release or the expression of this joy. True joy cannot be contained any more than the fountain can refuse to shoot skyward once the water has gone through the pump. The issue is not "will we" express joy, but "how will we" express this glorious joy.

For Reflection
1. What is the connection between mercy and joy?
2. If our joy is not the result of our religious activity or our spiritual knowledge, what is the cause of our great and glorious joy?
3. Contrast mercy and grace. Is one superior to the other?

Endnotes
1. Vern McLellan, *The Complete Book of Practical Proverbs and Wacky Wit*, Copyright © 1996 by Tyndale House Publishers, Inc. Wheaton, IL.
2. Ibid., George Eliot.
3. Martin Luther, *Leadership*, Vol. 9, No 1.

Section 3

The Expression of Joy

15

Joy Expressed in Rejoicing

"And on that day they offered great sacrifices, rejoicing because God had given them great joy…" (Nehemiah 12:43, NIV).

Everybody wants joy. Most persons endeavor to produce a level of joy in their lives, but the maximum they attain is a measure of happiness. Joy, as we have seen, is not the result of good works or even of conscious effort. True joy is a gift from God. We read that *the disciples were filled with joy and with the Holy Spirit* (Acts 13:52, NIV). This was a gift given by Christ and received by the disciples. So it is with us!

In this division of the book we will look at the expression of joy, for joy received, but unexpressed, would be well-nigh impossible. It should be as difficult for us to receive God's joy without showing it as it would be for a dog to be happy without wagging his happiness indicator—his tail.

In my analogy of the fountain, I've suggested that joy is the pump and the dancing plumes of water are a response to the action of that pump. God is the energizing source of our joy, but as long as our emotions remain in the pump, they will never be expressed. They need to be released as a beautiful dancing fountain of joy.

I've sought to establish that joy is a noun—it is a real substance. The release of that joy—its expression in life—is characterized by the verb *rejoice*. This word occurs in our English Bible nearly 200 times in 187 separate verses, and the noun form of the word, *rejoicing*, appears 29 times in 29 verses. If we add the 90 times the adjective *glad* appears, we have 318 words for the expression of joy in contrast to the 158 times the word *joy* appears. This means that we see joy being expressed two times more frequently than we see it being commanded. This is to be expected, for one pump can spew water through many fountainheads.

What It Means to Rejoice

In the Old Testament, the Hebrew word most used for *rejoice* is *samach*. W.E. Vine tells us, "*Samach* occurs about 155 times in the Old Testament . . . The verb *samach* suggests three elements: (1) a spontaneous, unsustained feeling of jubilance, (2) a feeling so strong that it finds expression in some external act, and (3) a feeling prompted by some external and unsustained stimulus."[1]

Samach rejoicing is not a theological treatise on the goodness of God. It is a spontaneous display of emotion as a response to the stimulus of God's presence and performance. It is far more than a mere feeling; it is a vivacious expression of that feeling. It is most likely to be exuberant, physical, and even boisterous. Others do not need a hearing aid to be aware of this release of joy. Very likely it can be heard, seen, and sensed all at the same time.

Looking at the New Testament words for joy, Lawrence O. Richards tells us the following:

> There are three different word groups in the NT that express the idea of joy. *Agalliao* is a loud, public expression of joy in worship. It focuses attention on God and His past and future work for the believer.
>
> *Euphraino* emphasizes a community joy, expressed by believers in times of religious festival or neighborly banquet. It does not describe the feelings of the individual as much as the atmosphere of shared enjoyment.
>
> *Chairo* is the word for joy that is used most often in the NT. It has reference to both the subjective state of joy and the things that bring joy. Each of these words is used in the Septuagint to translate several of the Old Testament terms for joy. The New Testament retains the basic Old Testament outlook on joy.[2]

A powerful example of the use of *chairo* is after the resurrection of Jesus. The women who came to the empty tomb were commanded by the angel to go and tell Christ's disciples what they had seen. As they went, Jesus met them with the greeting, *"'Rejoice!' So they came and held Him by the feet and worshiped Him"* (Matthew 28:9*b*, NKJV). Other translations say, *"All hail"* (KJ), and *"Greetings"* (NIV), but the word *chairo* fundamentally means "rejoice!" Christ was both the cause for rejoicing and the object of their rejoicing, for they immediately bowed, grasped His feet, and worshiped Him. They vigorously and physically expressed their feelings.

Whether the rejoicing be the *agalliao* loud, public expression of joy in worship, the *euphraino* rejoicing that emphasizes a community joy expressed by believers in times of religious festival, or the *chairo* rejoicing that embraces both the subjective state of joy and the things that bring joy, any of these forms of joy could disrupt many church services on Sunday. If the angels in heaven rejoice and shout when a person gives his or her life to Christ, why should we be denied the same joy and a similar expression of that joy here on earth? The expression of joy is natural; it is the repression of joyful feelings that is wholly unnatural, even if it is religious.

Action, Command, Response

REJOICE is an action, for verbs give action to nouns. When Jesus made His triumphal entry into Jerusalem, *"...the whole multitude of the disciples began to rejoice and praise God with a loud voice for all the mighty works that they had seen; Saying, Blessed be the King that cometh in the name of the Lord: peace in heaven, and glory in the highest"* (Luke 19:37-38). They did not stand aside in meditation. They loudly rejoiced and praised God—proclaiming Jesus their King.

REJOICE is also a command. Paul required the believers to, *"Rejoice with those who rejoice; mourn with those who mourn"* (Romans 12:15, NIV). This does not sound like a suggestion; it is a command. God is not pleased with our mere "feeling" of joy. He wants it expressed in rejoicing. A non-rejoicing Christian is living in disobedience to God.

REJOICE is, of course, a response. Paul reported, *"But even if I am being poured out like a drink offering on the sacrifice and service coming from your faith, I am glad and rejoice with all of you"* (Philippians 2:17, NIV). Paul's response to the demands made on him by ministry to the saints was not regret or remorse. It was rejoicing. The way that we respond to life and its demands is a choice made by us, as is the way we react to the ministry God has given to us.

Release of an Attitude of Heart

REJOICE is a release. The prophet reported, *"I delight greatly in the LORD; my soul rejoices in my God. For he has clothed me with garments of salvation and arrayed me in a robe of righteousness, as a bridegroom adorns his head like a priest, and as a bride adorns herself with her jewels"* (Isaiah 61:10, NIV). Joy in God's provision and positioning of our lives builds up an inner pressure that needs release. The pump has compressed our feelings. Release them in rejoicing! Let your joy spring forth like a fountain of water. Such deep feelings must be released or they will do internal damage. Sometimes a grouch is nothing more than a person who has never learned to rejoice.

REJOICE becomes a repetition. The joy received is repeated when released as rejoicing. David realized this, for he sang, *"Be glad in the LORD, and rejoice, ye righteous: and shout for joy, all ye that are upright in heart"* (Psalm 32:11). The more he expressed his joy, the greater it became. Shouldn't that work for us as well?

REJOICE is a wonderful verb. It is often expressed melodiously, and other times it is released in pageantry. Sometimes it is released in vocal praise, even with a loud shout. Rejoicing is a release of an attitude of heart that lets the outside know what is going on inside. It becomes a window to the heart. While the prophet said, *"The heart is deceitful above all things, and desperately wicked: who can know it?"* (Jeremiah 17:9), I believe that the redeemed saints of God often find that the heart is gloriously joyful even in the midst of very negative circumstances. It can rejoice because of a relationship with God, even when relationships in life are unpleasant and threatening. In rejoicing, we find what God has produced in our hearts.

REJOICING has God as its object and is an act of our will. None of the benefits of rejoicing can be experienced until we choose to release the divine joy God has placed within us in rejoicing. We repeatedly hear the writers of the Scriptures say *"I will rejoice...."* Almost anyone can rejoice when deep joyful emotions are stirred, but since God's joy is resident in us through the presence of the Holy Spirit and His abiding fruit, we can determine to rejoice.

REJOICING is an effect; God and His works are the cause. Rejoicing does not produce the joy, but it provides the key to release it. Sometimes we think that going through the motions we used in the past when we released divine joy will produce that joy again. It won't. We can sing the same songs, shout the same shouts, and even dance the same dance without producing joy. Never forget that *rejoice* is a verb that gives expression to the noun *joy*. We receive the joy from its divine source. We release that joy in human rejoicing.

God Rejoices Over Us

Those who may feel that rejoicing is a bit irreligious need to know that God rejoices over us. The prophet informs us, *"The LORD thy God in the midst of thee is mighty; he will save, he will rejoice over thee with joy; he will rest in his love, he will joy over thee with singing"* (Zephaniah 3:17). If God can rejoice over us with joy and singing, surely we can rejoice over God with joy and song. God can't consider irreligious what He consistently does—rejoice.

When the prophet foresaw God's plan to return the people of Judah to their own land, he heard God say, *"I will rejoice in doing them good and will assuredly plant them in this land with all my heart and soul"* (Jeremiah 32:41, NIV). God not only does good things for and to His people, He rejoices in doing so. He expresses His deep inner joy at keeping His covenants with us. How wonderful it would be if God's people would do His bidding with a rejoicing spirit. It is a joy to serve the Lord, and all that service should be with rejoicing.

REJOICE was Paul's favorite praise word: *"Rejoice in the Lord alway: and again I say, Rejoice"* (Philippians 4:4). Because God's joy is resident in us, we should always rejoice in the Lord, and we should rejoice in the Lord in all possible ways. The concluding chapters of this book will deal with some of these wonderful ways we can rejoice in the Lord—like having a time of celebrating God!

For Reflection

1. If rejoicing is not a theological treatise on the goodness of God, what is it?

2. Is the rejoicing of a congregation all together pleasing to God? If so, why don't we do it more often?
3. Rejoice is equally a command, a response, and a release. Give one Bible example of each of these.
4. Make it a point today to rejoice over what God has done for you and who He is: a totally righteous and awesome Creator who perfectly loves you.

Endnotes

1. *Vine's Expository Dictionary of Biblical Words*, Copyright © 1985, Thomas Nelson Publishers, Nashville, TN.
2. Lawrence O. Richards, *Expository Dictionary of Bible Words*, Copyright © 1985, 1991 by Zondervan Corporation, Grand Rapids, MI.

16

Joy Expressed in Celebration

"...their sorrow was turned into joy and their mourning into a day of celebration" (Esther 9:22, NIV).

Earlier I quoted Lawrence O. Richards in saying, "The New Testament retains the basic Old Testament outlook on joy."[1] Readers of the Old Testament will have to admit that the worship of the Hebrews was filled with celebration. They celebrated their feasts, their seasons, their rituals, their coronations, their dedication ceremonies, and many more activities. If, indeed, the New Testament retains the Old Testament outlook on joy, we must embrace celebration as an expression of our joy. How wonderful that this is a valid form of rejoicing!

The Old Testament provided for far more feasts than fasts. Three of these feasts—the feasts of Tabernacles, Passover, and Pentecost—were compulsory for every Hebrew male to attend. Their feast days were extensive family reunions with exceedingly happy fellowship. Once they were assured that their sacrifice had been accepted at the Brazen Altar and their sins had been covered by the sprinkled blood, the rest of their time in Jerusalem was a joyful celebration. To them, a holy day was a happy day. It should still be so for us.

Leander Keck shares the following insightful observation:

> I do not know why so much of mainline Protestantism has become a joyless religion. Perhaps we are more impressed by the problems of the world than by the power of God. Perhaps we have become so secular that we indeed think that now everything depends on us; that surely ought to make us depressed. Perhaps we have simply gotten bored with a boring God whom

we substituted for the God of the Bible.

We sometimes sing the Doxology as if it were a dirge. Even the Eucharist, despite the words of the Great Thanksgiving, is rarely the thankful, joyous foretaste of the Great Banquet with the One who triumphed over Death, but mostly a mournful occasion for introspection. A joyless Christianity is as clear a sign that something is amiss as a dirty church.[2]

In a Spiritual Rut?

What's wrong with really celebrating God? Each service need not be like the preceding one. There will, of course, be times when the Spirit is dealing with sin and sinners, but not always. Happily there will be other times when the Holy Spirit seeks to induce an atmosphere of celebration in the whole congregation. It might even get a little noisy, but it will be joyful noise. Who said that silence is golden in the sight of God? What is so sacred about sameness? Frankly, "Worship without creativity is like inviting a congregation to come and chew on Kleenex for an hour."[3]

Some of the conferences I have been invited to are billed as a "Celebration." They are often spiritual funfests. They have processionals with banners and marching musicians. The singers and dancers fill the stage with joyful motion and song. Sometimes the entire congregation is given small flags to wave as the worshipers sing praises unto God. The entire atmosphere is jubilant. Joy is the keynote of the hour. The worship sessions are actually fun.

I have often heard speakers at these conferences declare that such actions as we were enjoying would be inappropriate in local churches. Why? Can joy be expressed only in neutral auditoriums in a convention atmosphere? I agree that such behavior would go against the normal ritual of most churches, but maybe we need to get out of our ruts and celebrate God with joyful hearts.

Kenneth Latourett, an excellent historian, wrote: "Once Christianity became legal in the Roman Empire the faithful got doctrinal, conformist, and creedal and sent the church into 1,000 years of uncertainty...Martin Luther got the movement unstuck when he rediscovered grace. Then conservatives codified God and liberals deified humans and gummed it up again."[4]

Oh, how quickly spontaneity is overwhelmed with sacrament and service. Perhaps it is the security of sameness that makes ritual so acceptable. Could it be that we want to be able to worship without having to think or feel? Conversely, maybe we want to have the same feeling every church session?

Rev. Roberts offers this analysis:

> Just like do's-and-don'tism, liturgism comes in two varieties: high and low…If you're from Bumpkin Ridge you may need a different strategy than genuflections and incense. It's the old favorite hymns that make you feel the religion in your heart…And it's not the priest crossing himself that makes you feel religious, but the thump of his fist on the pulpit, and the song leader flingin' his arms every which way. If there isn't enough arms-flingin' and Bible-thumping, the Holy Spirit just doesn't grip on you…If the high liturgy was a French dinner, this is a hot dog and a Coke.[5]

Whether we are pipe organ devotees or keyboard and guitar aficionados, we all risk falling into a formal ritual that is lifeless and not actually expressive of our current feelings about God. We need to remember that we do not gather to see or be seen. We gather to celebrate God, for joy is easily and perhaps best-expressed in celebration sessions.

A Jubilant Celebration

In the preceding chapter, we looked at what W.E. Vine says about the most common Hebrew word for "rejoice." "The verb *samach* suggests three elements: (1) a spontaneous, unsustained feeling of jubilance, (2) a feeling so strong that it finds expression in some external act, and (3) a feeling prompted by some external and unsustained stimulus."[6] There can be no doubt that *samach* rejoicing was made for celebration, and David knew how to *samach* celebrate God.

After the kingdom was established under him, David determined to bring the Ark of the Covenant to the Holy City. He did so in two distinct celebrations separated by about three months. In the first processional, he returned the Ark on a new cart as far as the threshing floor of Obed-Edom. We read, *"David and the whole house of Israel were celebrating with all their might before the LORD, with songs and with harps, lyres, tambourines, sistrums and cymbals"* (2 Samuel 6:5, NIV).

God showed His dissatisfaction with the means of transporting the Ark, so David had a study made of the provision of the Law. He found that the Ark was always to be carried on the shoulders of consecrated priests. Armed with this knowledge, David called for a second celebration march. The Bible describes them as holding nothing back in their attempt to please their God.

> *When those who were carrying the ark of the LORD had taken six steps, he sacrificed a bull and a fattened calf. David, wearing a linen ephod, danced before the LORD with all his might, while he and the entire house of Israel brought up the ark of the LORD with shouts and the sound of trumpets. As the ark of the LORD was entering the City of David, Michal daughter of Saul watched from a window. And when she saw King David leaping and dancing before the LORD, she despised him in her heart* (2 Samuel 6:13-16, NIV).

What a worship celebration! Singing, dancing, instrumental music, worship sacrifices every six paces, and loud shouting accompanied with the trumpet, and all this was unto the God of Israel.

Celebrating or Criticizing

There are two extreme contrasts in the story. First, David stripped off his kingly robes and wore the linen ephod of a priest. He was aware that all attention needed to be focused on God, for this was His celebration, not David's. David knew what John the Baptist later taught, *"He [Jesus] must increase, but I must decrease"* (John 3:30). True joyful celebration must be focused on Jesus, not anyone else. All celebrants become equal as worshipers. Only Jesus is the great one.

Second, we see David's wife, Michal, looking out the window as a non-participant, despised her husband for his exuberant behavior. David was worshiping in joyous humility, and Michal needed to know that joy does not come by observation, but by participation. It is not our intellectual comprehension of God that fills us with joy. It is His voice, His presence, and His indwelling Spirit that induce such joyful celebration responses.

Charles R. Swindoll wrote, "God is no distant deity but a constant reality, a very present help whenever needs occur. So? So live like it. And laugh like it! [The apostle] Paul did. While he lived he drained every drop of joy out of every day that passed."[7]

It is difficult, if not impossible, to criticize and to celebrate simultaneously. We need to get off the judgmental line and join the celebrants. When we stop leaning out the window as an observer and march in the procession with the worshipers, we'll understand what Solomon meant when he wrote, *"The fear of the LORD is a fountain of life"* (Proverbs 14:27a). The Hebrew word he used that we have translated to "fear" is *yirah*. Elsewhere in the Bible, we translate this word "reverence." Reverential worship, even the noisy, demonstrative worship of a celebration, becomes a fountain of life in our souls.

Celebrating the God Who Loves Us

Perhaps we see so little true celebration of God because we are so unaware that He is present and has been working on our behalf all week long. We don't realize that the ark of His presence is among us and the power of His Name has stood against our enemies day and night.

After describing the enthusiastic expressions of sports fans, Rod Cooper says, "I'm not saying that when you come to church you need to give each other high fives or do cartwheels down the aisle, but worship is a time of anticipation and expectation. We come together because all week God has been knocking home runs and scoring touchdowns in our lives. Worship is a time to celebrate what God has done for us."[8]

Philip Yancy says, "Like a victorious locker room, church is a place to exult, to give thanks, to celebrate the great news that all is forgiven, that God is love, that victory is certain."[9]

Of course, we'll be quietly solemn for funerals, but at all other times we need to recognize joyfully that Jesus is alive! He is present when we gather, and that very presence should stir a spirit of celebration in us.

When we watch the world respond so exuberantly to the stimuli happiness brings—such as in sporting events—and contrast this to the stoic solemnity evidenced in many churches, it becomes difficult to believe that true happiness comes from relationship with God. The concept of

God is so serious that few persons realize just how joyful a relationship with Him can be.

Henrietta Mears asks, "Are you proving that the Christian life is a joyful, happy thing? Do you look glad that you are a Christian? Does your life radiate joy and enthusiasm? Check yourself carefully on this before you teach it. Make the Christian life contagious."[10]

When we gather, we should celebrate God. Celebrate life. Celebrate Christian fellowship. Celebrate health and God's provision for healing. That was God's original purpose for gathering people together in the great feasts, and the Bible says, *"I the LORD do not change"* (Malachi 3:6a, NIV). Our gatherings need to be joyful times of fellowship with God and with His children.

This was the view of the psalmist who sang, *"One generation shall praise thy works to another, and shall declare thy mighty acts"* (Psalm 145:4). Isaiah was also an exponent of celebration, for he wrote: *"And you will sing as on the night you celebrate a holy festival; your hearts will rejoice as when people go up with flutes to the mountain of the LORD, to the Rock of Israel"* (Isaiah 30:29, NIV). Even Jesus participated in celebration, for in preparation of the Last Supper, He sent disciples into the city with instructions, *"Go into the city to a certain man and tell him, 'The Teacher says: My appointed time is near. I am going to celebrate the Passover with my disciples at your house'"* (Matthew 26:18, NIV).

If you still have difficulty with the concept of celebrating God, please cancel your reservations for the Marriage Supper of the Lamb in heaven. That will be a celebration beyond anything ever seen here on earth. We might feel more comfortable there if we had a few celebrations here in which to practice.

If the psalmists, prophets, and Jesus believed in and participated in spiritual celebrations, why shouldn't we? We can have a wonderful time expressing our joy in our Heavenly Father through music and the dance.

For Reflection
1. The Old Testament worship was full of celebration. Why is there so little real celebration in America's churches?

2. I say, "It is difficult, if not impossible, to criticize and to celebrate simultaneously." If you sit with David's wife in the window, watching celebration, what is likely to be your attitude?

3. List at least five things we can celebrate when we gather for worship.

4. What do you associate with celebrations you have enjoyed? Isn't the victorious Christian life worth celebrating? Be glad in the Lord.

Endnotes

1. Lawrence O. Richards, *Expository Dictionary of Bible Words*, Copyright © 1985, 1991 by Zondervan Corporation, Grand Rapids, MI.

2. Leander Keck in "The Church Confident," *Christianity Today*, Vol. 41, No. 1.

3. Cal LeMon in *Leadership*, Vol. 7, No. 2.

4. Quoted by Lloyd H. Alhem in "The Covenant Companion" (Aug. 1986), *Christianity Today*, Vol. 32, No. 7.

5. Robert Roberts in the *Reformed Journal* (Feb. 1987), *Christianity Today*, Vol. 33, No. 14.

6. *Vine's Expository Dictionary of Biblical Words*, Copyright © 1985, Thomas Nelson Publishers, Nashville, TN.

7. Charles R. Swindoll in "Laugh Again," *Christianity Today*, Vol. 37, No. 13.

8. Rod Cooper, *Preaching Today*, Tape No. 108.

9. Philip Yancey in *Leadership*, Vol. 8, No. 3.

10. Henrietta Mears in "Dream Big: The Henrietta Mears Story," *Christianity Today*, Vol. 40, No. 5.

17

Joy Expressed in Music

"Shout for joy to the Lord, all the earth, burst into jubilant song with music" (Psalm 98:4, NIV).

Music has its origins in heaven, not on earth. As a matter of fact, "Music is almost all we have of heaven on earth."[1] From the creation of the earth until saints are seen in heaven, God's heavenly home seems to have been filled with music. It is a vehicle for the expression of love and joy.

In my book, *Worship As David Lived It*, I write:

> In speaking to a rebellious people, God said, *"Behold, My servants shall sing for joy of heart, But you shall cry for sorrow of heart, and wail for grief of spirit"* (Isaiah 65:14, NKJV). The secret of joy lies in the relationship of the individuals to God. Self-will brings sorrow, while submission to God's will brings songs of joy. Those who are trying to "live their lives for Jesus" usually have more sighs than songs, but those who allow Jesus to live in their lives have shouts of joy that must be expressed.

> It is to be expected then, that one of the psalmists would sing out, *"Oh, send out Your light and Your truth! Let them lead me; Let them bring me to Your holy hill And to Your tabernacle. Then I will go to the altar of God, **To God my exceeding joy**; And on the harp I will praise You, O God, my God"* (Psalm 43:3-4, NKJV, emphasis added). When God is our "exceeding joy," our responses to Him will be joyful responses. Perhaps outward singing, shouting, leaping, and dancing will again release our inner joy as we worship the One who has lifted us from the darkness and weight of sin into the light and joy of His own countenance.[2]

Inducing and Releasing Feelings

Remember, it was God who said, *"My servants will sing out of the joy of their hearts…"* (Isaiah 65:14, NIV). The King James Version says, *"sing for joy…"* which may suggest we would sing to obtain joy in our hearts, but the New International Version correctly says, *"Sing out of the joy of their hearts."* God has implanted the joy. He expects to hear that joy released in song. It is not so much that God commands this; it is that He knows we cannot contain His joy. It must find expression, and song is such a natural expression of inner joy.

Music performs two main functions. It can induce feelings and it can release feelings. Our generation may be more aware of the first function—inducing feelings. The world has long known the power of music to control. Businessmen create moods with background music in their stores and offices. They learned long ago about the power of music to sell products and to create a "yes" attitude in the buyer. Satan, who seems to have been the music director of heaven, has prostituted music to induce persons to indulge in lust, drugs, and even violence. Music is a powerful force to introduce thoughts, feelings, and attitudes, and our mortal enemy, the devil, uses music masterfully.

William Booth, founder of the Salvation Army, said, "Secular music, do you say, belongs to the devil? Does it? Well, if it did I would plunder him for it, for he has no right to a single note of the whole seven. Every note, and every strain, and every harmony is divine and belongs to us. So consecrate your voice and your instruments. Offer them to God, and use them to make all the hearts about you merry before the Lord."[3] The Salvation Army, perhaps more than any other religious group, has used music as a force for the spreading of the Gospel of Jesus Christ.

Listening to Music

It seems likely that no generation has had more music available to hear than this present generation. With radio, television, recorded music, and an abundance of electronic musical instruments, we are surrounded by music that only kings could enjoy a few generations ago. But for all this music, we have become listeners of music far more than performers of music. We pay to attend concerts to hear others sing and play. People carry CD and cassette players and portable radios with them to listen to music. Conceivably they are putting into their heads what they lack in their hearts. At the highest level, they are identifying with the music and musician, but there is no creativity or joyful expression in the mere listener.

The music we listen to with enjoyment is indicative of what is going on inside us. Mahalia Jackson observed, "Anyone who sings the blues has a broken spirit...Being oppressed or worried about something and not knowing God, they've sought a way of trying to relieve themselves...the blues make you feel moody and sad and make you cry."[4]

Sometimes when I hear what others are enjoying as music, I feel sorry for them. What torment must be stirring in them. What hopelessness, what lust, what violence must fill their souls! Christians should take inventory of their musical tastes, for it will indicate what is dominant in their inner being.

United Singing

If the first function of music is to induce feelings, the second and divine purpose for music is to release our inner joy. God said that His servants would *"sing out of the joy of their hearts."* God knew that the joy He would impart to His creatures was too strong a force to be expressed in prose or liturgy, so He gave us songs to help us release our emotions along with our concepts. In doing so, He gave us a vehicle that allows believers with different backgrounds and totally different spiritual experiences to join together in expressing their joy in the Lord. That vehicle is music—especially singing and even more especially, united congregational singing.

United singing offers us several advantages. First of all, it causes us to join with other believers in expressing our faith. Second, it gives us a tailor-made vocabulary that helps us crystallize our thoughts and release our feelings. Third, congregational singing helps to release our emotions Godward instead of being repressed inwardly. Little wonder, then, that any religious movement that repressed singing never lasted a full generation. God has imparted a song and we must sing or burst!

With so little emphasis on participation in music in our culture, many persons sit or stand silently in our churches during vocal worship times. "I can't sing well" is their excuse. Donald Hustad comments, "Somehow, about forty percent of church goers seem to have picked up the idea that 'singing in church is for singers.' The truth is that 'singing is for believers.' The relevant question is not, 'Do you have a voice?' but 'Do you have a song?'"[5]

Songs of the Redeemed

The final book of the Bible is filled with the songs of the redeemed. Graham Kendrick shares a valuable observation:

> Interestingly, of all the songs in the book of Revelation, not one is a solo. The twenty-four elders sing and cast their crowns before His feet, the united voices of countless angels resound, every living creature in heaven and earth and under the earth and all that is in them are joined in one song. Those who are victorious over the beast are given harps and a song to sing. In every case, multitudes of people or angels unite in the same song with absolute unity.[6]

Think about it. We will not listen to the trained vocalist in heaven; we will be the vocal participants in worshiping God in song.

The prophet declared, *"The ransomed of the LORD will return. They will enter Zion with singing; everlasting joy will crown their heads. Gladness and joy will overtake them, and sorrow and sighing will flee away"* (Isaiah 51:11, NIV). In the New Testament, Zion becomes a type for the Church. God declared that the ransomed would come into the true Church with singing as an expression of the everlasting joy that fills their souls. There is no better way to overcome sorrow and sighing than singing with joy in our hearts. No matter what life may have dealt to us, Jesus has given us a divine joy that is far greater than any negative in life could ever be. As we sing forth that joy, especially with others, the whole atmosphere of our lives changes. Music allows the inner joy to have a glad outward expression.

The great composer, Franz Joseph Haydn, said, "When I think upon my God, my heart is so full of joy that the notes dance and leap from my pen; and since God has given me a cheerful heart, it will be pardoned me that I serve him with a cheerful spirit."[7]

If it seems to you that I am overemphasizing the place of music, especially singing to release the joy God has deposited in each of the redeemed, please note that I am merely taking my place with Martin Luther. He said, "Next to theology, I give to music the highest place and one of the most magnificent and delightful presents God has given us."[8]

Music in the Scriptures

Singing and playing musical instruments is a major topic in the Bible, for singing is mentioned 287 times, and playing instruments unto the Lord is noted 317 times. This is far more frequent than all the basic Bible doctrines put together are mentioned. Musical expression has to be important to God for Him to talk so much about it. "Music is God's best gift to man; the only art of heaven given to earth; the only art of earth we take to heaven."[9]

Paul taught that singing was the point of overflow of the Holy Spirit within us. He wrote: *"Do not get drunk on wine, which leads to debauchery. Instead, be filled with the Spirit. Speak to one another with psalms, hymns and spiritual songs. Sing and make music in your heart to the Lord"* (Ephesians 5:18-19, NIV). God equates the Spirit-filled life with song—old songs, new songs; united singing, private singing; songs with others, songs for others. Just release the Spirit in song, for He is a singing Spirit.

As a personal testimony, Paul said, *"What is the conclusion then? I will pray with the spirit, and I will also pray with the understanding. I will sing with the spirit, and I will also sing with the understanding"* (1 Corinthians 14:15, NKJV). The Living Bible puts it: *"Well, then, what shall I do? I will do both. I will pray in unknown tongues and also in ordinary language that everyone understands. I will sing in unknown tongues and also in ordinary language so that I can understand the praise I am giving."*

Singing in Worship

One of the most beautiful and relaxing ways to release joy is extemporaneous singing in the Spirit. Like a joy-filled child at play, making up a song as he or she sings it, we can release our spirit melodiously, with the

Holy Spirit providing the words in a language so unknown to us that our conscious mind cannot censor it. For years, I have made it a daily practice to sing in the Spirit as part of my morning worship time.

Singing is such an important part of the expression of joy that I marvel at churches that often have difficulty getting sufficient singers to form a choir or instrumentalists to make up an orchestra. What a privilege this is! What a chance for a united releasing of joy! What a worship incense to offer unto God! In the last church I pastored, we had three choirs—adult, youth, and children—and the size was limited by the capacity of our choir loft. We would probably never have won a state prize for our singing, but the joy released from the singers lifted the congregation into greater heights of worship expression to God.

Quite obviously, not all religious singing is worship or a release of joy. Only the music that is birthed in the Spirit of God and/or is sung or played directly to God will fulfill this calling. Too much of the singing and instrumental playing are performance-oriented and call attention to the musician rather than to God. This may be beautiful, but it does not release joy. It may induce happiness, but that is about all. We need to *sing and make melody in our hearts TO THE LORD.* (See Ephesians 5:19.)

While heaven may have no solos, earth has many of them. The religious scene today is filled with vocal and instrumental music. There are some excellent ensembles whose music stirs praise and the release of joy. The secret to letting these musicians express your joy is to inwardly join with them. Sing in your heart along with the singers. Let your spirit join the instrumentalists and emotionally participate in the music. Otherwise, you will merely be an observer as others release their joy.

Consider also that we are enjoined to *"sing unto the Lord"* seventeen times in the King James Version. The psalmists were both proclaimers and practitioners of this instruction. They said, *"O come, let us sing unto the LORD: let us make a joyful noise to the rock of our salvation. Let us come before his presence with thanksgiving, and make a joyful noise unto him with psalms"* (Psalm 95:1-2). I am quite certain that if we obey this instruction, our mouths will not be the only part of our bodies involved in singing. Our hands, feet, and body will join in unless we deliberately restrain them.

For Reflection

1. Where did music originate?
2. Music performs two main functions. It can _____feelings, and it can _____feelings.
3. List three advantages of united singing of praise.
4. Include songs of praise in your devotions or at different times throughout the day. You'll find this a stress-reliever and a joy-inducer.

Endnotes

1. Joseph Addison (1672-1719), Entry 7900, *Draper's Book of Quotations for the Christian World*, Edythe Draper, Copyright © 1993, Tyndale House Publishers, Inc., Wheaton, IL.
2. Judson Cornwall, *Worship As David Lived It*, pages 94-95, Copyright © 1990 by Destiny Image, Shippensburg, PA.
3. William Booth, "*William and Catherine Booth*," Christian History, No. 26.
4. Mahalia Jackson (1911-1972), Entry 7900, *Draper's Book of Quotations for the Christian World*, Edythe Draper, Copyright © 1993, Tyndale House Publishers, Inc., Wheaton, IL.
5. Donald Hustad, *Leadership*, Vol. 3, No. 1.
6. Graham Kendrick, *Leadership*, Vol. 15, No. 2.
7. Franz Joseph Haydn (1732-1809), Entry 7931, *Draper's Book of Quotations for the Christian World*, Edythe Draper, Copyright © 1992, Tyndale House Publishers, Inc., Wheaton, IL.
8. Ibid., Martin Luther (1483-1546), Entry 7914.
9. Ibid., Letitia Elizabeth Landon (1802-1838), Entry 7904.

18

Joy Expressed in Motion

"Rejoice in that day and leap for joy, because great is your reward in heaven" (Luke 6:23, NIV).

Religion seems to love David's statement, *"Give ear to my words, O LORD, consider my meditation"* (Psalm 5:1). When we assemble together for worship, I sometimes think we almost talk God to death. Our public gatherings are very word-centered. We talk to one another, we pray repeatedly to God, and the preacher talks continually to the people. He is pleased if the people will at least say an *"Amen!"* back to him.

This same David—who was good with words—with the help of a few other inspired songwriters, lists at least nine ways to express joy to the Lord. Three of these affect <u>the mouth</u>:

1. **Vocal praise:** *"I will bless the LORD at all times: his praise shall continually be in my mouth"* (Psalm 34:1).
2. **Singing:** *"So will I sing praise unto thy name for ever"* (Psalm 61:8*a*).
3. **Shouting:** *"Let thy saints shout for joy"* (Psalm 132:9*b*).

Three of these are expressed by <u>the hands</u>:

4. **Lifting the hands:** *"I will lift up my hands in thy name"* (Psalm 63:4*b*).
5. **Clapping the hands:** *"O clap your hands, all ye people"* (Psalm 47:1*a*).
6. **Playing musical instruments:** *"Sing unto him with the psaltery and an instrument of ten strings"* (Psalm 33:2*b*).

The final three means of expressing joy to God involve <u>body posture</u>:

7. **Standing:** *"Ye that stand in the house of the LORD, in the courts*

of the house of our God...sing praises unto his name; for it is pleasant" (Psalm 135:2-3).

8. **Dancing:** *"Thou hast turned for me my mourning into dancing: thou hast put off my sackcloth, and girded me with gladness"* (Psalm 30:11).

9. **Kneeling and bowing:** *"O come, let us worship and bow down: let us kneel before the LORD our maker"* (Psalm 95:6).

(Further references to these actions are in other Psalms. A concordance will give them to you.)

The standard Old Testament word for joy is *samach.*

> The emotion expressed in the verb *samach* usually finds a visible expression. In Jeremiah 50:11, the Babylonians are denounced for being glad and *jubilant* over the pillage of Israel. Their emotions are expressed externally by their skipping about like a threshing heifer and neighing like stallions. The emotion represented in the verb (and concretized in the noun *simchah*) is sometimes accompanied by dancing, singing, and playing musical instruments. This was the sense when David was heralded by the women of Jerusalem as he returned victorious over the Philistines (1 Samuel 18:6). [1]

It seems that God, our Maker, realizes we need to communicate from our entire being. The release of joy cannot be confined to words, for heaven's joy involves our emotions and emotions seldom fit our vocabularies.

Communicating by More than Words

Religion seems to confine our joyful responses to words, but not everyone is capable of expressing inner emotion with words alone. That is the job of a poet. At a conference in Albuquerque, New Mexico, I taught on the value of releasing our joy through body language. When I was through, the pastor expressed his disapproval of my teaching. He declared that we worship God through words alone, and that all body gestures were worldly and out of place. All the while he was criticizing my message, he was widely gesturing with his hands, walking from one side of the pulpit to the other, nodding his head, and alternately pointing to the congregation and to me. He emphasized his message with very obvious body language. He couldn't even condemn my message on the use of body language without using that very language. I smiled at the contrast between what his mouth said and what his body revealed.

If we communicate with one another through body motions that dramatize our feelings and the meaning of our words, shouldn't we do the same thing when sharing our joy with the Lord? Watch persons talking on a cell phone. Even when in public, they often gesture quite widely although they surely realize that the person to whom they are speaking cannot see any of their body motions. These movements are part of our daily speech pattern. All of us have learned to communicate with a combination of words and actions.

Why do we become so abnormal when we gather to express the wonderful joy God has given to us? What's wrong with a little body action in church?

A Variety of Expressions

On a recent Sunday, my pastor put this message on the first page of the church bulletin:

> You'll soon notice that we are a *worship center!* Whether singing, praising, bowing, kneeling, clapping, or dancing, we love to worship! We invite you to join in your personal expression of honor to our God. We *stand* and *raise our hands* in adoration and submission to Him; we *clap our hands* in jubilation and celebration of His goodness to us; we *bow our heads and bend our knees* in reverence and recognition of His greatness. Some will even *dance* in joy.
>
> There are many expressions of *praise* and *worship*. The most important issue is that you touch God. We will not be offended with your method of worship and ask that you allow that same freedom to those around you. Just let everything be done decently and in order as worship unto our worthy heavenly Father![2]

I am proud that my pastor grants this liberty to the worshipers. Because this is my home church, I can tell you that not everyone does everything as they worship, but everything does get done. Not everyone stands, all do not sing, the shouters are in the minority, and very few persons dance, but these expressions will all be part of the Sunday worship session.

That is one of the values of united worship. Perhaps nothing has stifled true expression of joy more than our desire for uniformity and conformity. The divine joy in our hearts must be expressed variously and vigorously or it soon becomes religious ritual. Why should everyone have to do the same thing at the same time? Is there an unhealthy desire to maintain control of the expressions of joy?

Look at your own family. The same joyful event will elicit different responses from the children. Some of this difference is based on personality traits, some on the physical state, and still other responses are enhanced or restricted by past experience and teaching. Isn't this also true of the family of God? Persons will respond differently, but when given the liberty, joy will be expressed. Even if religion has trained persons to remain silent, the facial muscles, like the wagging tail of a dog, will give away the inner joy.

Body: Temple of the Holy Spirit

For several years, I taught pianists to play the organ "evangelistic style." Some of the books I used were from Mel Bay Music Publications. Imagine my delight to find that the president of the company had written a book on worship in which he shares the following teaching:

> ...we must overcome the notion that to be spiritual is to deny the body. For a long time we have harbored the notion that the body is somehow bad and that movement of the body, even something as simple as lifting hands, is ugly and fleshly. Instead, we must affirm that the body is the temple of the Holy Spirit, and there is beauty and grace in worshipping God with our bodies. To deny the use of the body in worship is similar to trying to put air into a balloon that cannot be expanded... Scriptures have many accounts of people worshipping God with their bodies. This even includes dancing.[3]

My youth was spent in the Pentecostal movement where there was great freedom in expressing our joy through body movements. Unfortunately as I grew older, I walked with my denomination out of that freedom into the bondage of reducing religious expressions to words, spoken and sung. When God sent a missionary to my church who began to urge people into greater freedom, I had a difficult time with it. I'm embarrassed to admit how bound I was in my spirit. As I visited around, saw the glorious freedom others were enjoying, and sensed the high level of joy that was being expressed, I set my heart to return to worshiping God with my entire being—body, soul, and spirit. My personal liberty released my congregation into a greater freedom of expression and divine joy became paramount in our services.

My greatest difficulty was with the dance, for the training in my youth depicted all dancing as sensual and carnal. As I spoke at conferences where they had interpretive and even choreographed dancing, I saw how it could lift the spirits of the congregation of people to a great exuberance of joy. I also saw dancers weeping in joy before the Lord, and I had to admit that they had as much right to use their bodies to express their joy as I had in using my mind and mouth. From time to time, dance teams would dance onto the platform, take my hand, and involve me in a simple dance. When I got over my embarrassment and abandoned my thoughts to enjoying God, I found a glorious flow of joy and delight in dancing before the Lord.

I have made it a practice for many years to include a little dance in my morning devotion time. It gets me out of the "Dr. Cornwall" mood and returns me to my childhood before God.

Becoming Like Little Children

Whatever else Jesus had in mind when He said, *"I tell you the truth, unless you change and become like little children, you will never enter the kingdom of heaven"* (Matthew 18:3, NIV), I believe He was telling us that we need to be as uninhibited as small children when we try to express our joy in the Lord. Watch children skip for sheer joy. How long has it been since you've seen an adult do that? Children will hug, clap, sing, dance, and just jump up and down to release their inner joy, and they don't seem to care how they are dressed or who is watching.

Oh, that God would help us return to such innocence. We've become so sophisticated that we are out of touch with our real feelings, and when those feelings overwhelm us, we don't remember how to release them. We need to become childlike again.

In some conferences, leaders have encouraged various responses that released pent-up joy. Sometimes this has been as simple as having all of us raise our hands, and then wave them back and forth as we sang. That simple physical gesture released the expression of joy in many persons. At other times we've been encouraged to do a simple side-step dance while clapping our hands. A few leaders have taught us to sign a chorus in the language of the deaf. These are all elementary, but they represent a beginning, and provide a wonderful release of joy. We need to do something to get motion back into the expression of our emotions.

I've seen a great welling up of joyful expressions when persons were encouraged to bring their offering to the front rather than have ushers come and take it. As persons walk down the aisle waving their offering in the air, it often produces a release of inner joy, encouraging a little dance, a soft shout, and sometimes even a laugh. Doesn't this eat up a lot of time? Yes! But it also frees some persons to express their joy in the Lord.

I've seen joy released in the simple act of having people join hands and sway while singing a love song to Jesus. There is something in the community action that makes it safe to release joy.

You say, "We could never do that in our church!" Why not? Is your religious code set against expressing joy? We've been solemn for so many years that we need to balance it out with joyful expression. This will force us to go beyond mere words. Maybe we should remind ourselves how we express our pleasure at the ballpark or in the stadium when our team is winning.

Are We Really Excited?

True excitement will demand body action to gain a full expression. Is it possible that we are no longer excited with Jesus? Has our gathering together on Sunday already become a cold ritual, so emphasizing the holiness of God that we forget the wonderful joy Jesus brought to us at our salvation? Of course God is holy, but He has made that holiness available to us. He said, *"Be ye holy; for I am holy"* (1 Peter 1:16*b*). This is a commitment. Because He is holy, we, too, can be holy by the indwelling of God's Holy Spirit. Holiness does not come by our action, but by our acceptance of God's provision. That, alone, should inspire such a joyful feeling as to cause us to clap our hands and maybe even move our feet a little.

Joy needs an honest expression from our entire redeemed being. It is even expressed in humor and laughter.

For Reflection
1. Why cannot the release of joy be confined to words?
2. Think about the contrast between being child-like and childish in our worship.
3. True excitement will demand physical motion to gain a full expression. List at least five ways body movement can release the excitement of joy. (Next time you have your devotions, feel free to use some of them!)

Endnotes
1. *Vine's Dictionary of Biblical Words*, Copyright © 1985 by Thomas Nelson Publishers, Nashville, TN.
2. Dr. Jim Cornwall, Scottsdale Worship Center, Scottsdale, AZ, April 11, 1999.
3. William Bay, *The Beauty of Worship*, pages 161-162, Copyright © 1984 by Mel Bay Publications, Inc., Pacific, MO.

19

Joy Expressed in Mirth

"Our mouths were filled with laughter, our tongues with shouts of joy..." (Psalm 126:2).

You may fault me for the use of the word *mirth*, for the dictionary defines it as follows: "gladness or gaiety as shown by or accompanied with laughter."[1] According to this definition, mirth doesn't sound very "religious," but it is very real. I am using the word in the widest sense of expressed joy.

The Living Bible translates the words of the prophet, *"These, the ransomed of the Lord, will go home along that road to Zion, singing the songs of everlasting joy. For them all sorrow and all sighing will be gone forever; only joy and gladness will be there"* (Isaiah 35:10, TLB). If, as I have suggested earlier, Zion is a type or symbol of the Church, God says our journey should be joyful and filled with gladness.

In one of His ironically humorous statements, Jesus said, *"And whenever you fast, do not look dismal, like the hypocrites, for they disfigure their faces so as to show others that they are fasting. Truly I tell you, they have received their reward"* (Matthew 6:16, NRSV). They suppose that for religion to be genuine, it has to be dull and without joy. Their reward? *They succeed!* They look and probably feel dismal. What irony! Let's not mimic them.

This is not God's will for His redeemed children. He has provided joy and gladness for us on our journey from earth to heaven. We don't need to falsify a sober, somber attitude toward life. Christ didn't. The early Christians didn't. We shouldn't! Jesus said, *"I have come that they may have life, and have it to the full"* (John 10:10*b*, NIV). Let's live life to the fullest.

We don't have to await our entrance into heaven to enjoy Christ's provision and imparted life. We can have joy in the here and now, and that joy should be expressed in humor and even playfulness.

Alex Lowe, the renowned mountain climber, when asked whom he considered the best mountain climber to be, said, "The best climber in the world is the one who's having the most fun."[2] Somehow I feel that could be said of Christians. The best Christian is probably the one who's having the most fun, for when we thoroughly enjoy what we are doing, we do it with intensity, indomitability, and insatiability.

Playing?

Speaking in the voice of wisdom, which many see as a euphemism for Jesus, Solomon wrote, *"Then I was the craftsman at his side. I was filled with delight day after day, rejoicing always in his presence, rejoicing in his whole world and delighting in mankind"* (Proverbs 8:30- 31, NIV). Is this a picture of God the Father and God the Son enjoying both the act of creation and the results of the creative act?

My son-in-law, Norbert Senftleben, is an architect by profession, but a linguist by hobby. He was reading this passage from Proverbs in the French Bible and noticed that the word we translate as "rejoicing" is "*playing*" in the French Bible. This so startled Norbert that he asked the Lord about "playing" before him.

The next day an architect who speaks French joined his office, and Norbert spent the whole day speaking French with him. "We had a ball!" he told me. That evening the Lord said to him, "Now you know what playing is. Playing is an activity that you thoroughly enjoy."

Serving God should inherently be "playing." It is far more than a duty; we should so enjoy it that it becomes our delight and joy! We can talk His language to Him all day long as we go about our daily duties. We can enjoy His companionship with us in all of our activities. Life can become a joy-filled playing with Jesus. It will bring us back to our childhood.

Priming the Joy Pump

Life needs some humor in it. Mack McGinnis said, "After God created the world, He made man and woman. Then to keep the whole thing from collapsing, He invented humor."[3]

Do I dare impose this modern proverb on the Christian world? Christ Jesus makes us new men and women through the new birth, and He places us in a new world—the Church. To keep this from collapsing, He brings in humor. He said, *"...he that is of a merry heart hath a continual feast"* (Proverbs 15:15).

I do not believe God has given us humor to produce joy, for all true joy has its origins in God Himself. I do believe that humor often opens our hearts to let the joy out, for humor opens the emotions. In my youth, many of us did not have running water in our homes. We were dependent upon a well with a hand pump. If the pump had not been used for a while, it often lost its prime and had to have some water poured into the top to create suction. We called this "priming the pump." I believe that is what humor often does. It enables us to pump up some of the joy in our souls that is so needed in our outer life.

A serious student of the Gospels must admit that Jesus used humor as a teaching aid. He wasn't stoic or sad, for people liked to be around Him. Christ used paradox as humor. What could be more paradoxical or funny than *"the blind leading the blind"*? It doesn't take much imagination to hear a giggle flow through the crowd of listeners. Similarly, when He spoke of a camel going through the eye of a needle, these common folk could understand this preposterous statement as humorous.

The most common type of humor Christ used was irony. The ironical is always marked with a subtle sharpness of insight, free from the desire to wound. This is what distinguishes it most clearly from *sarcasm*. There is definite irony in Christ's question, *"Are grapes gathered from thorns, or figs from thistles?"* (Matthew 7:16b, RSV).

The Therapy of Humor

Laughter is healing. Josh Billings says, "Laughing is the sensation of feeling good all over, and showing it principally in one spot."[4] Not long ago I allowed myself to get overly burdened with the problems of persons I had counseled. They may have left my study feeling better, but I was miserable. The weather was good and I chose to sit on my patio overlooking the cactus garden I planted a few years ago. Just sitting, staring almost blankly, I felt and then heard a deep laugh rumble up and explode uproariously. It was followed by a few calmer chuckles. It was as though the tension in my soul had been short-circuited and disappeared in an instant. I was released to God's joy. This has happened to me repeatedly. God gives me a good laugh and I am restored to emotional health. Not by accident does the Word tell us, *"A merry heart doeth good like a medicine"* (Proverbs 17:22a).

Heinrich Heine reminds us, "Laughter is wholesome. God is not so dull as some people make out. Did He not make the kitten to chase its tail?"[5] My favorite portrait of Christ hangs on the wall in front of my computer. It is called "Jesus Laughing." He has His head tilted back, His mouth open, and His eyes squinted in an obvious peal of laughter. Jesus, who came to bring us joy, lived a joy-filled life that included laughter. As a matter of fact, Joseph Addison tells us, "If we may believe our logicians, man is distinguished from all other creatures by the faculty of laughter."[6]

The distinguishing characteristic of the Toronto revival is laughter. As the presence of God sweeps across the congregation, persons laugh almost uncontrollably. This is distressing to some observers and has become the brunt of much criticism in pulpits across the world, but many persons are healed emotionally and some physically in the tremendous release this laughter brings to them. I think that God is telling His Church here on earth, "Go ahead and laugh. Stop taking yourself so seriously." We're not going to get out of this world alive anyway, so why borrow its troubles and anxieties as though they were eternal values? Lighten up and enjoy Jesus while you breathe in and out.

Joy: A Testimony to Freedom

There is an interesting passage of Scripture in a historic book of the Old Testament that relates to this. God's people had returned from Babylonian captivity to rebuild the destroyed Temple. Ezra called the people together to read the Law to them, and had interpreters put it into the language the people had learned in Babylon. The instant guilt it produced brought the people to sorrow, mourning, and weeping. Both Ezra and Nehemiah told the people, *"This day is holy unto the Lord your God;*

mourn not, nor weep…" (Nehemiah 8:9*b*).

What followed was probably as much a surprise to them as it is to many modern Christians. *"Then he said unto them, Go your way, eat the fat, and drink the sweet, and send portions unto them for whom nothing is prepared: for this day is holy unto our Lord: neither be ye sorry; for the joy of the LORD is your strength"* (Nehemiah 8:10). Fundamentally, they were told that rejoicing should follow repentance. God wants us to be sorry for our sins only long enough to confess and forsake them. Then He wants us to return to the joy of living as freed persons.

The best French and Spanish translations render *"the sweet"* as wine that was mixed with spices. One wonders if God preferred to have His people a little tipsy than overcome with sadness and guilt.

Bible students realize that wine in the Old Testament was considered an elixir of joy. It was always a part of Jewish festivities, and its fundamental purpose was to cause persons to lose their inhibitions and enjoy life around them. God wants to do this for us by means of His Holy Spirit.

My Argentine son-in-law was raised in a strict religious society. His father, although a businessman, was also a preacher. He educated his son in a military academy, which further inhibited the expression of his feelings. When he was baptized in the Holy Spirit, he testifies that he went into uncontrollable laughter—sidesplitting laughter—for about two hours. He was so uninhibited by the joy of the Spirit that he could come out of himself and enjoy life.

Filled with the [Holy] Spirit

Paul put this into perspective when he wrote, *"And be not drunk with wine, wherein is excess; but be filled with the Spirit"* (Ephesians 5:18). The wine of the Old Testament was but a type of the Spirit of the New Testament. God's Holy Spirit was given to release us from our cultural inhibitions to enjoy the flow of God's wonderful joy in our everyday lives. Even Christ's first miracle—turning water into wine at a marriage feast in Cana—became a visual demonstration of His willingness to keep the joy flowing.

Some have said this laughter and joyful expression is for the new converts. Don't forget that we never stop laughing because we are old. We grow old because we stop laughing.

Applying the Old Testament injunction that repentance should be followed by *"eating the fat and drinking the sweet,"* we enter into the flow and life of the Holy Spirit until all self-incrimination, self-doubt, and deep inhibitions are overcome. We can then respond easily and fully to the joy of the Lord. Our coming together can become festivals. Our sorrow can be turned into joy. The wise man said, *"Go thy way, eat thy bread with joy, and drink thy wine with a merry heart; for God now accepteth thy works"* (Ecclesiastes 9:7).

When we can express our joy in mirth and pleasure, we will be qualified to minister in the joy of the Holy Spirit.

For Reflection
1. Is humor really necessary in a Christian's life? Explain.
2. In many places where revival has come, laughter is overtly evident. Is this the result of God, man, or the devil?
3. Look around you. God is not so dull as some people imply. Point out at least five things in life that cause you to believe God has a sense of humor. (Please don't use a mirror.)

Endnotes
1. *Webster's Seventh New Collegiate Dictionary*, Copyright © 1971, G.& C. Merriam Company, Springfield, MA.
2. *Bits & Pieces*, Rob Gilbert, Ph.D., Editor, Copyright © 1999 by The Economics Press, Inc., Caldwell, NJ
3. Ibid.
4. Josh Billings, *The Speaker's Source Book of 4,000 Illustrations*, compiled by Eleanor L Doan, Copyright © 1960 by Zondervan Publishing House, Grand Rapids, MI.
5. Ibid., Heinrich Heine.
6. Joseph Addison, *The Spectator*, No. 494. Quoted in *Dictionary of Quotations* collected by Bergen Evans, Copyright © 1978 by Avenel Books, New York, NY.

20

Joy Related to Ministry

"He…will return with songs of joy, carrying sheaves with him"
(Psalm 126:6, NIV*).*

The word *minister* can be used either as a noun or a verb. In today's religious society, we are more prone to use it as a noun. We have reduced the term "minister" to the office of the full-time professional clergy. Webster's dictionary supports this definition. The question, "Are you a minister?" usually means "Are you a pastor?" Please allow me to broaden this term to Biblical proportions, for the word *minister* is a verb all through the Old Testament. It was not an office; it was an activity. The priests served the people. They ministered on their behalf.

Ministry and minister in the Bible are terms referring to service performed by believers. Paul affirmed this when he wrote, *"And he gave some, apostles; and some, prophets; and some, evangelists; and some, pastors and teachers; For the perfecting of the saints, for the work of the ministry, for the edifying of the body of Christ"* (Ephesians 4:11-12). The New International Version uses the word *service* instead of ministry. These offices (or officers) of the Church are provided to prepare and equip believers for service—ministry. This call to service is universal. Christ has provided a ministry for each of us. What a privilege! What a joy! Imagine being *"…workers together with him…"* (2 Corinthians 6:1).

The Example of Our Lord

Jesus illustrated service to others, taught us to serve others, and commanded us to minister to others. Christian service is not optional—it's a command. We are pardoned from sin, but we are not excused from service. Did He place such emphasis on our service because He is short-handed? Are we better servants than the angels? Of course not! Christ knew that our ministry to others would be a key to releasing our joy. We are invited to minister to others because it so gloriously benefits us.

"Life is a place of service," Leo Tolstoy said. "Joy can be real only if people look upon their life as a service and have a definite object in life outside themselves and their personal happiness."[1] Jesus said of Himself, *"For even the Son of Man did not come to be served, but to serve, and to give his life as a ransom for many"* (Mark 10:45, NIV). Remember that this same Jesus told us, *"I tell you the truth, anyone who has faith in me will do what I have been doing. He will do even greater things than these, because I am going to the Father"* (John 14:12, NIV). Christ's goal for His Church was the continuation of His ministry of service. He wants His redeemed children to be available to Him for ministry to others.

Charles Spurgeon wrote the following concerning service:

I thought I looked and saw the Master standing, and at his feet lay an earthen vessel. It was not broken, not unfitted for service, yet there it lay, powerless and useless, until he took it up. He held it awhile, and I saw that he was filling it, and soon I beheld him walking in his garden, where he had "gone down to gather lilies." The earthen vessel was yet again in his hand, and with it he watered his beautiful plants and caused their fragrances to be shed forth more abundantly. Then I said to myself, "Sorrowing Christian, hush! Hush! Peace, be still! You are this earthen vessel, powerless, it is true, yet not broken, still fit for the Master's use. Sometimes you may be laid aside altogether from active service, and the question may arise, what is the Master doing with me now? Then may a voice speak to your inmost heart, 'He is filling the vessel, yes, only filling it to be ready for use.' Don't ask how he will use you. Be silent. Is it not all too great an honor for you to be used by him at all? Be content, whether thou art employed in watering the lilies or in washing the feet of the saints. It doesn't really matter. Surely it is enough for an earthen vessel to be in the Master's hands and employed in the Master's service."[2]

The Glorious Joy in Service

If service was an expression of Christ's joy, it can also be a glorious expression of our joy. This is not automatic, unfortunately. Far too much Christian service is offered grudgingly out of a duty response, or it is performed professionally without expressed feeling.

Mother Teresa, so known for her ministry to the poor and suffering said:

> I very often tell the Sisters to approach the poor with joy, knowing that they have plenty of reason to be sad. They don't need us to confirm their sadness for them.
>
> We are committed to feed Christ who is hungry, committed to clothe Christ who is naked, committed to take in Christ who has no home—and to do all this with a smile on our face and bursting with joy.[3]

Ministry that flows out of joy will become service with a smile! Rejoicing service! Service that does not flow out of joy has its own penalty. Remember what God said through Moses, *"Because you did not serve the LORD your God joyfully and gladly in the time of prosperity, therefore in hunger and thirst, in nakedness and dire poverty, you will serve the enemies the LORD sends against you. He will put an iron yoke on your neck until he has destroyed you"* (Deuteronomy 28:47-48, NIV). When we lose our joy in ministry, we will serve our enemy of resentment, pride, and selfishness. May God help us to always serve others joyfully and gladly.

As a boy I was taught that joy is spelled Jesus Others You. Jesus must have first place in our lives and service. Out of that will flow ministry to others and, ultimately, there will be ministry and spiritual service to our own individual lives.

Our first ministry, then, is unto Jesus. Three times the Bible instructs us, *"Give unto the LORD the glory due unto his name"* (1 Chronicles 16:29a; Psalm 29:2a; 96:8a). Three is the number of witness in the Bible. God gives us a triple witness of our responsibility to ascribe to Him the glory that is due Him. We do this in praise, worship, and obedience to His Word.

Praising Joyfully

It is so easy to express our praise and worship—whether in song, vocal expression, the dance, or other ways—joyfully. Actually, it is difficult to sing mournfully to God when His joy is welling up in our spirits. God delights in joyful songs. He delights when everything we offer Him is done with a cheerful spirit. Jesus went to the cross with joy. Surely we can go to church with great joy.

When David appointed special Levites to praise the Lord as representatives of the people of Israel, *"David spake to the chief of the Levites to appoint their brethren to be the singers with instruments of music, psalteries and harps and cymbals, sounding, by lifting up the voice **with joy**"* (1 Chronicles 15:16, emphasis added). David's call was not merely for excellence or volume. He insisted that the singing and playing of instruments be a release of joy. How glorious it is that we can minister unto Jesus with the very joy He has imparted to us!

The psalmist sang, *"Blessed is the people that know the joyful sound: they shall walk, O LORD, in the light of thy countenance"* (Psalm 89:15). The Living Bible puts it, *"Blessed are those who hear the joyful blast of the trumpet, for they shall walk in the light of your presence."*

The trumpet was used to call for a solemn assembly. It was the call to worship. When we minister unto the Lord with great joy of heart, we are rewarded with the light of God's presence. In the Old Testament, this was the Shekinah—the glory cloud. Few things we do can make us more aware of God's radiant presence than expressing our worship in a joyful manner. God shines when we sing!

Lifting Others' Spirits

If the second letter of joy stands for **Others**, then not only is ministry unto God an expression of our inner joy, all ministry to other persons can equally be done with joy. Whether we minister to physical needs or spiritual needs, our service should flow out of our fountain of joy. We can sometimes be charitable with such a sense of personal guilt or obligation as to make the recipient feel put down. How much better it is to share with such joy as to lift the spirit of the other person to our level of joy.

If God has blessed you and you choose to share what you have with another, do it with great joy, not from a sense of duty or obligation. The joy you share may prove to be more valuable than the money or service that you give. It is not by accident that the Bible tells us, *"Each man should give what he has decided in his heart to give, not reluctantly or under compulsion, for God loves a cheerful giver"* (2 Corinthians 9:7, NIV).

One area of ministry to others that so often lacks joy is the operation of vocal gifts in our churches. So often the interpretation of tongues, prophecy, and even the preaching is condemnatory, negative, and fearful in its tone. If, as is purported, this is God speaking to us through human instrumentality, why does He sound so angry, disturbed, or dismayed? He is a joyful God and He thoroughly enjoys His children. Of course, He will correct us, but He doesn't have to get angry to do so.

Paul taught, *"...everyone who prophesies speaks to men for their strengthening, encouragement and comfort"* (1 Corinthians 14:3, NIV). We must let this communication come through us joyously. We all learn better when the communication is happy and pleasant. Harshness and condemnation tends to induce fear that closes our spiritual ears.

When I was a pastor, I categorically rejected any prophetic utterance that had a whiplash of condemnation in it. I would publicly say, *"'God did not send his Son into the world to condemn the world, but to save the world through him'* (John 3:17, NIV), therefore I doubt that he sent you to condemn us. We do not receive this message as coming from God."

The problem is seldom with the message; it is with the messenger. Sometimes as I have preached through a translator, the harshness in the spirit of the interpreter so tainted what I was saying that the audience received wrong impressions. Basically, the interpreter said what I was saying, but he or she let his or her own spirit color the message. The fears, anxieties, or unbelief of the interpreter came through stronger than the message I was seeking to convey.

Letting God's Joy Flow through Us to Others

I believe this sometimes happens when we try to communicate God's message to others. God's message gets colored, stained, and tainted by our fears, preconceptions, and unbelief. The longer I live, the greater my belief that if we cannot speak God's Word with joy, we would do well to keep silent in the church.

When we are assembled together, the exercise of the vocal gifts of the Spirit is not our only means of ministry. Often we are given opportunity to pray for the sick and distressed who are standing close to us. We can do this with great joy. Entering into the suffering of the one for whom we are praying is not necessary. We help the sick person to enter into the joy of God's provision for healing.

A Christian hug that releases joy sometimes lifts the person we hug out of depression and sorrow and gives them a feeling of being loved and of belonging. Similarly, if we are counseling another, we should let God's joy flow. The person we counsel may have severe problems, but God has serious answers, and they are joy producing when they are received and acted upon.

Ministry to others can be exhausting and unrewarding, but when we are bubbling with the joy of the Lord as we minister, we find a refreshing and a renewing in our own spirits. It is not the response of the person to whom we minister that gives us strength—*"The joy of the LORD is your strength"* (Nehemiah 8:10*b*). There is no way we can give out all of the joy that Christ is putting in us, but the harder we try, the greater the flow of joy. Every time we splash another with joy, we get wet with the same joy.

Joyful Ministry to Self

The third portion of the acrostic *Jesus Others and You* is **You**. We need to learn how to minister to ourselves with joy. Far too often we minister to ourselves out of condemnation or, at the best, out of duty. Sometimes, we have ministered to others to such a point of exhaustion that we have no energy left with which to minister to ourselves.

Henry Nouwen says this,

> We have fallen into the temptation of separating ministry from spirituality, service from prayer. Our demon says: "We are too busy to pray; we have too many needs to attend to, too many people to respond to, too many wounds to heal. Prayer is a luxury, something to do during a free hour, a day away from work or on a retreat..." But to think this way is harmful... Service and prayer can never be separated; they are related to each other.[4]

Not only does personal prayer suffer by being neglected, it suffers by being offered in negative, whining ways. We so often verbalize our fears instead of our faith. We complain about our pains and disappointments rather than rejoice in God's faithful provision. On occasion, we enter into prayer in some level of victory and end up in complete defeat because we did not release God's joy when we spoke to the Lord. Joyful prayer becomes powerful prayer. Joyful prayer ascends to the throne of God. Joyful prayer lifts our spirits from the morass of everyday living and gives us a season in a heavenly atmosphere.

Similarly, reading the Bible is more than a religious discipline. God's Book should be read as a love letter from home. It is the instruction book for our lives. Martin Luther said, "The Bible is alive, it speaks to me; it has feet, it runs after me; it has hands, it lays hold of me."[5] The Bible can be approached and read joyfully. It will not only become a source of our joy; it can be a marvelous channel for the release of our joy.

For many Christians, reading the Bible has become an unpleasant chore. Few modern Christians have ever read it through from Genesis to Revelation, even though they embrace it as God's Word to them. "If you are religious, it is easier to read some pious book than the Bible. The Bible treats you like human life does—roughly."[6]

We desperately need to minister to ourselves in daily Bible reading for, "We have never truly breathed air nor seen light until we have breathed in the God-inspired Bible and see the world in the Bible's light."[7]

Furthermore, as we daily read God's Book, we get a progressively enlarged and corrected image of Christ Jesus. David Livingstone testified, "All that I am I owe to Jesus Christ, revealed to me in his divine book."[8] What a joy this revelation of Jesus will become to us on a daily basis, and that great joy will be expressed to Him in worship.

For Reflection
1. If we confine the word "minister" to its verb form, what does it refer to?
2. How can service be an expression of Christ's joy?
3. If **J O Y** is viewed as an acrostic, how does it demonstrate the order of our service?

Endnotes

1. Leo Tolstoy, *Leadership*, Vol. G/No.22, The Economics Press, Inc., Fairfield, NJ.

2. Charles Haddon Spurgeon, *The Quotable Spurgeon*, Copyright © 1990 by Harold Shaw Publishers, Inc, Wheaton, IL.

3. Mother Teresa, *In My Own Words*, Copyright © by José Luis Gonzalez-Balado, published by Random House Value Publishing, Inc., New York, NY.

4. Henri J. M. Nouwen, Entry 10211, *Draper's Book of Quotations for the Christian World*, Edythe Draper, Copyright © 1992 by Tyndale House Publishers, Inc., Wheaton, IL.

5. Martin Luther, *Martin Luther—The Early Years*, Christian History, No. 34.

6. Oswald Chambers, *Christianity Today*, Vol. 37, No. 11.

7. Fyodor Dostoevsky, *Christian Reader*, Vol. 33, No. 5.

8. David Livingstone, *Christian Reader*, Vol. 33, No. 5.

21

Joy Expressed with Worship

"My lips will shout for joy when I sing praise to you—I, whom you have redeemed" (Psalm 71:23, NIV)

The word *worship* means different things to different persons. Even *Webster's Collegiate Dictionary* uses an inch and a half of space in trying to define the word both as a noun and as a verb. My favorite Webster definition is, "to regard with extreme respect, honor, or devotion."

Worship is an attitude to some persons. They feel they must be in a pious mood to worship or they equate quietness with worship. Sometimes they claim introspection as a worship experience. At other times, they define a sense of awe as worship. I've heard persons declare that they had a great worship experience looking into the Grand Canyon. Maybe they did, but I strongly suspect that they were so overawed by the sight of magnificent grandeur that they defined their emotions as worship.

Other persons feel that worship is an action. They consider singing, standing, and raising their hands in church to be worship. If they bow their heads or kneel, they are certain that they have worshiped—maybe, but maybe not. Actions alone are not worship experiences. Actions may release worship, but they do not produce it. I have watched individuals do all of the "worship actions" during a service in a cold, calculated manner that spoke more of religious ritual than real worship.

Probably a combination of attitude and action comes closer to true worship—worship is an attitude expressed in physical action. It is the inner person seeking to communicate with God through the expressions of the outer person—the body. When awe of God is expressed as adoration of God, worship occurs. The inner feelings will vary and the outer expressions will be diverse, but as Erwin Lutzer says, "You don't learn to praise in a day, especially since you may have been complaining for years! New habits take time to develop. But you can begin today, and practice tomorrow, and the next day, until it becomes part of you."[1]

What Is Involved in Worship?

While praise is but the initial step in worship, we will not worship until we praise. Praise is something that we can initiate in our approach to God. Worship is what we do when we get into His presence. We need to set our minds to praise and worship God.

However, worship is not all mental—it is also emotional. We are inspired to worship by a display of God's love that stirs our emotions and motivates us to respond to God. In that response, we worship God with the body, soul, and spirit. The Old Testament equation, repeated in the New Testament is: "*And Thou shalt love the LORD thy God with all thine heart, and with all thy soul, and with all thy might*" (Deuteronomy 6:5). Matthew, Mark, and Luke all record Jesus as quoting this verse. This might indicate that merely singing a song with a congregation of believers is not true worship. More than the mouth needs to be involved for divine worship.

Roger Palms wrote:

Worship is not just personal introspection, or we would worship our feelings. Worship is not even a warm glow, or we would worship that. We worship One outside ourselves. We concentrate on him, we praise him, we adore him, we hear his Word for he is announcing it to us. We listen in holy awe to the word of God, for it is a part of that "all" of Scripture which is given by the out breathing of God and is personally necessary for "my" correction and "my" instruction in righteousness.[2]

Responding to His Love

Since worship involves all of our being and is expressed to the Almighty, simple definitions are difficult. In most of the twelve books I have written on worship, I share my personal definition of worship: "*Worship is love responding to love.*" I don't think this is an oversimplification. It defines the two chief ingredients of worship: response and love.

While praise to God can be initiated by us, worship is actually initiated by God. We may praise the Lord from a distance, but we can only worship when conscious of the presence of the Lord. Praise, emotion, and even association with other praisers may bring us to a God consciousness, but we will not truly worship until we sense a flow of His love to our hearts.

Worship is almost an involuntary response to a revelation of God. Heathen kings in the Old Testament worshiped Jehovah when there was a manifestation of His presence and power. If idolaters worshiped when God drew near, surely we Christians will do so, too.

If Psalm 100 is a pattern for our worship responses, we will, *"Enter into his gates with thanksgiving, and into his courts with praise: be thankful unto him, and bless his name"* (Psalm 100:4). In the imagery of the Mosiac Tabernacle, we enter the Outer Court with thanksgiving, the Inner Court with praise, but we stand before the veil that forms the partition into the Holiest of Holies and in response to the divine presence, we *"bless his name."* We worship! We respond to His person rather than merely to His performance.

Worship, then, is not an Outer Court activity where the issues of sin are settled at the Brazen Altar and the Laver. Worship is performed in the Holy Place in front of the veil where the Altar of Incense was installed. True worship flows to God when we are in His recognized presence. It is a response, a reaction, and almost a repercussion.

The Blending of Love, Joy, and Worship

This shouldn't seem so strange to us, for life, as we live it, illustrates this. It is difficult to receive a loving hug without giving one in return. When someone says, "I love you," our almost involuntary response is, "I love you, too." Love received almost demands to be given back.

Love and worship are coupled together all through the Bible. Interestingly enough, love and joy are also blended. *"But the fruit of the Spirit is love, joy, peace...."* (Galatians 5:22). David knew this connection for he sang, *"Let them also that love thy name be joyful in thee"* (Psalm 5:11b). In the love relationship of worship, joy flows as a by-product.

How grateful I am to God that the Holy Spirit brings Christ's love into our lives as a channel for His joy. The order is love, then joy. It is likely that this love becomes the producer of the joy, and when we release that joy back to the object of our love, it becomes worship of God. Worship, then, is giving back to God what we have received from Him—love. It is love *responding* to love. Having used this definition of worship in a dozen of my books, I now realize that it would be better stated, "Worship is love *joyfully* responding to love." Tim Keller tells us, "Our emotions become worship when, in response to a truth about God, we give something back to God."[3] Love for God is not worship until we express it back to Him joyfully.

We've already seen that in the Old Testament wine is viewed as an elixir of joy. It is not by accident, then, that the beautiful love poem, The Song of Solomon, starts out with, *"Let him kiss me with the kisses of his mouth—for your love is more delightful than wine"* (Song of Solomon 1:2, NIV). Some persons have difficulty in accepting this book—feeling it is too sensual to be spiritual. Actually, however, it is a beautiful analogy of our relationship to Jesus Christ. It pictures the courtship and marriage of Christ to His bride, the Church. It is a joyful time of getting to know the object of our love.

A Joy-Producing Love Relationship

If worship is love joyfully responding to love, the coming together of two lovers is a beautiful picture of worship. This book does not consider the responses of the lovers as a duty, but as a delight. The lovesick maiden cries out, *"Take me away with you—let us hurry! Let the king bring me into his chambers. We rejoice and delight in you; we will praise your love more than wine. How right they are to adore you!"* (Song of Solomon 1:4, NIV).

These are extremely joyful expressions to the King. So should our worship be. Reading Solomon's song in a prayerful attitude and identifying with the love-struck maiden can, in itself, become a worship experience. It is obvious that she is enjoying this love relationship. It is a joyful time for her. Why not let worship be a joyful time for us as well?

When, in chapter three, there was a brief separation, the maiden cried, *"I will get up now and go about the city, through its streets and squares; I will search for the one my heart loves. . . . Scarcely had I passed them when I found the one my heart loves. I held him and would not let him go till I had brought him to my mother's house, to the room of the one who conceived me"* (Song of Solomon 3:2, 4 NIV).

Being joyfully in love with Jesus, we will not allow times of separation to be prolonged. We will do whatever it takes to get back into a joyful fellowship with Him. We, as she, will discover that He is not difficult to find. Through the prophet Jeremiah, God said, *"You will seek me and find me when you seek me with all your heart"* (Jeremiah 29:13, NIV).

Worship for Our Own Sake

Thomas Aquinas, a medieval theologian, wrote, "We pay God honor and reverence, not for his sake (because he is of himself full of glory to which no creature can add anything), but for our own sake."[4] God will survive if we never worship Him, but we won't. Our worship of God does not make Him joyful—He is inherently joy filled. Worship of God allows us to release the heavenly joy He has instilled in us, and that very release of joy is fulfilling to our whole being.

I don't believe I have ever been more joyful than during a season of true worship of God. At times it seems that every fiber of my being tingles with ecstasy after a love session with Jesus. It is fulfilling and extremely satisfying, but it does not satiate my desire for God. As Eugene Peterson says, "Worship does not satisfy our hunger for God; it whets our appetite."[5]

Just as our maiden in the Song of Solomon couldn't seem to get enough time with her lover, so we feel that life continues to infringe upon our love relationship with Jesus. As an older gentleman used to repeatedly testify in my father's church, "I'm satisfied with an unsatisfiable satisfaction." I did not understand this in my youth, but having lived many years in a love relationship with Jesus, I can honestly say "Amen!" His love gets sweeter the longer I serve Him, and my joy is more intense the longer I worship Him.

I have declared that joy is expressed in rejoicing, celebration, musical expression, physical motion, mirth, and ministry, but there is no higher expression of joy than true worship of our Lord. It is almost the difference between holding hands on a date and enjoying the lifetime commitment of marriage. The deeper our involvement with the love of Christ, the greater the release of our joy as we worship Him.

In His Arms

Tim Keller reminds us, "In order for us to worship, our mind, will, and emotions have to be moved."[6] What can more quickly do this than being in the arms of Jesus? Remember that it was said several times of Jesus, *"He took the children in his arms, put his hands on them and blessed them"* (Mark 10:16, NIV). He still does! He offers us security, protection, and unqualified love. No wonder Jesus so stirs us to joyful worship.

Being around Jesus is always joy producing, but it should be obvious that living in Christ's presence fills us with continual joy. This is the glorious by-product of worship. The Psalmist knew this for he sang, *"I will dwell in the house of the Lord forever"* (Psalm 23:6*b*), and, *"My soul yearns, even faints, for the courts of the LORD; my heart and my flesh cry out for the living God...Blessed are those who dwell in your house; they are ever praising you. Selah"* (Psalm 84:2, 4, NIV).

This sounds quite eternal. We'll dwell in the house of the Lord *forever*, and we'll *ever* praise God. Expressing our joy through worship will not be limited to our time/space dimension. Christ has loved us with an everlasting love. This makes it possible for us to have an everlasting joy.

For Reflection

1. Worship is not all mental—it is also emotional. We worship God with the _____, _____, and _____.
2. In the love relationship of worship, what flows as a by-product?
3. If worship is love joyfully responding to love, the coming together of two lovers is a beautiful picture of worship. Give four ways a love-filled marriage illustrates worship.
4. In order to receive and share His joy with others, set aside daily time to worship God, as well as to read His Word and pray. You'll be gloriously blessed.

Endnotes

1. Erwin W. Lutzer (1941-), Entry 8747, *Draper's Book of Quotations for the Christian World*, Edythe Draper, Copyright © 1992 by Tyndale House Publishers, Inc., Wheaton, IL.
2. Roger Palms in "Living Under the Smile of God," *Christianity Today*, Vol. 34, No. 14.
3. Tim Keller, *Leadership*, Vol. 15, No. 2.
4. Thomas Aquinas, medieval theologian, *Men of Integrity*, Vol. 1, No. 1.
5. Eugene H. Peterson, *Leadership*, Vol. 16, No. 1.
6. Tim Keller, *Leadership*, Vol. 15, No. 2.

22

Joy Is Eternal

"Surely you have granted him eternal blessings and made him glad with the joy of your presence" (Psalm 21:6, NIV).

Gladness is impermanent and happiness is transient, but joy is eternal. The fleeting thrills the unbeliever seeks in this life go to the grave with him or her, but the joy that God gives to believers goes right into eternity with them. Just as joy is independent of earthly circumstances, its duration is unaffected by our departure from this earth and into the eternity God has prepared for us.

In saying that joy is eternal, we need to take at least a brief look at eternity. Quite frankly, our concepts of eternity are seriously limited because we've lived our entire lives in a time-space dimension. The longer we live, the less permanent anything seems to be. Life on earth is in a constant state of change, and our brief stay here doesn't give us sufficient time to keep up with all the changes. To think of eternity as being unchanging and everlasting doesn't fit our current frame of reference.

One thing we do know about eternity is that God dwells there. He declared, *"For thus saith the high and lofty One that inhabiteth eternity, whose name is Holy; I dwell in the high and holy place, with him also that is of a contrite and humble spirit, to revive the spirit of the humble, and to revive the heart of the contrite ones"* (Isaiah 57:15). If God lives there, we need not fear going to our Father's house, and this verse indicates His invitation to share His eternity.

We know also that eternity is timeless, limitless, and without beginning or end. A famous man said, "Eternity is the ocean; time is the wave."[1] Another declared, "In eternity everything is just beginning."[2] A third, in attempting to give us time-space creatures a point of reference, suggested, "High up in the north in the land called Svithjod, there stands a rock. It is one hundred miles high and one hundred miles wide. Once every thousand years a little bird comes to this rock to sharpen its beak. When the rock has thus been worn away, then a single day of eternity will have gone by."[3] May I add that our joy will still be sparkling like a fountain of water.

What Things Are Eternal?

Besides calling our joy eternal, the Bible, especially the New Testament, speaks of at least seven things we have touched here on earth that are eternal in nature and scope. It speaks of eternal glory (1 Peter 5:10), eternal inheritance (Hebrews 9:15), eternal redemption (Hebrews 9:12), eternal judgment (Hebrews 6:2), eternal salvation (Hebrews 5:9), God's eternal purpose (Ephesians 3:11), and God's eternal power (Romans 1:20). We have touched and been touched by all of these while on our pilgrimage, but we will know a limitless abundance of them when we are released from the ties of this earth.

A common expression in the religious circles in which I traveled in my youth was, "God gives us a little bit of heaven to go to heaven in." Fanny J. Crosby wrote a joy-filled hymn based on this, which Billy Graham has used as the theme song for all his crusades, *"Oh, what a foretaste of glory divine!"*[4] I think God gives us a foretaste to create a taste for heavenly things.

Eternity, eternal values, eternal life, and an eternal hope all lay the groundwork for the expression of our eternal joy. Certainly, in light of this contact with eternity, our joy will be eternal for at least five reasons.

Biblical Authority

First of all, the Bible calls our joy everlasting and eternal. Isaiah says, *"…everlasting joy shall be upon their head…"* (Isaiah 51:11). If God said it, that settles it! While Isaiah's prophecy directly referred to Israel's return to Jerusalem from captivity, there is a prophetic perspective in this verse—that is, it refers both to a near event and a future event. He wrote: *"The ransomed of the LORD will return. They will enter Zion with singing; everlasting joy will crown their heads. Gladness and joy will overtake them, and sorrow and sighing will flee away"* (Isaiah 51:11, NIV). This literally happened when the Israelites returned from Babylon to build the Temple in Jerusalem. We know this will be equally true when believers enter heaven because the book of Revelation shows this joy being expressed.

I like the way The Living Bible translates this verse: *"The time will come when God's redeemed will all come home again. They shall come with singing to Jerusalem, filled with joy and everlasting gladness; sorrow and mourning will all disappear"* (Isaiah 51:11, TLB). Some of God's redeemed will *"come home again"* through death. Month by month, I lose friends and acquaintances this way. They precede me into heaven with great rejoicing.

Others will *"come home again"* at the return of our Lord Jesus Christ, but either way, they will be *"filled with joy and everlasting gladness."* Our initial concept of heaven will be a family reunion as we are reunited with loved ones from whom we have been separated. What pleasure! What fadeless joy! Then we will enter into a personal relationship with Jesus far beyond anything we have been able to experience here in our time-space dimension. It will be like adding an additional pump to the fountain. More and more plumes of water will rise and fall in a cascade of everlasting joy, with no exhaustion to diminish the display.

The Gift of Eternal Life

A second reason we can consider our joy to be eternal is that the life Christ gave us is eternal. The Wise Man wrote, *"He has made everything beautiful in its time. He has also set eternity in the hearts of men; yet they cannot fathom what God has done from beginning to end"* (Ecclesiastes 3:11, NIV). God sets eternity in the hearts of believers.

Jesus greatly reinforced this when He said of believers, *"I give unto them eternal life; and they shall never perish, neither shall any man pluck them out of my hand"* (John 10:28). This is taught in several other New Testament passages, the most notable of them being John 3:16: *"For God so loved the world that he gave his one and only Son, that whoever believes in him shall not perish but have eternal life"* (NIV). The promise is not mere salvation, but the present gift of eternal life. We are not going to receive eternal life; we received it at our conversion.

If God has put eternity in our hearts, and if the result of the new birth at salvation is entering into eternal life, we become creatures of eternity while still living in the limitations of time. Only our physical bodies are restricted to this time-space dimension. As incredible as it seems, our spirits have already entered into eternity with God. No wonder the fountain of joy bubbles day and night in our inner spirit!

Maybe realizing that eternity already has a place in our life as a Christian, we can better understand some of the heavenly longings we experience. C.S. Lewis said, "If I find in myself a desire which no experience in this world can satisfy, the most probable explanation is that I was made for another world."[5]

Putting this together, we find the level of joy believers have in their lives is an eternal joy bubbling in the eternity of their spirits. It is a joy that was made for another world, but is being demonstrated in this world. It is a force from eternity that is being released in the dimension of time. When unbelievers refer to it as "unearthly," they are far more accurate than they realize. Our joy came from eternity and will go back into eternity with us.

As Sir Thomas Browne puts it, "The created world is but a small parenthesis in eternity."[6]

Eternity preceded creation and eternity will proceed long after this created world passes away. Gloriously, we have already entered into this endless realm at our conversion. When we step from this earthly kingdom to the eternal kingdom of God, there is nothing earthly that goes with us, but everything heavenly that we have received will flow endlessly into eternity; especially our joy.

A.W. Tozer comments, "How completely satisfying to turn from our limitations to a God who has none. Eternal years lie in his heart. For him time does not pass, it remains; and those who are in Christ share with him all the riches of limitless time and endless years."[7]

The Joy of an Eternal God

The third reason I'd consider our joy eternal is that the *source* of our joy is eternal. In the first section of this book, we declared that joy has its source in God the Father, God the Son, and God the Holy Spirit. The Bible declares that this God is eternal—*"The eternal God is thy refuge, and underneath are the everlasting arms"* (Deuteronomy 33:27*a*). If this source of joy is eternal, then joy itself must be eternal.

I also suggested that the Bible, God's kingdom, and God's presence are further sources of the joy that flows in the lives of believers. These are eternal, for we read that Jesus said, *"Heaven and earth shall pass away: but my words shall not pass away"* (Mark 13:31). Peter tells us, *"For so an entrance shall be ministered unto you abundantly into the everlasting kingdom of our Lord and Saviour Jesus Christ"* (2 Peter 1:11). Even in the Old Testament God promised, *"the LORD your God goes with you; he will never leave you nor forsake you"* (Deuteronomy 31:6*b*, NIV). If these sources of our joy are eternal in nature, the joy they introduce into our lives must be as eternal as these sources.

An Ever-flowing Fountain of Joy

A fourth reason our joy is eternal is because the flow of our joy is eternal—the fountain is not on a timer. When I sat in the lobby of the hotel in Fort Worth and watched the fountain that inspired this book, I was aware that it spewed its beautiful streams of water continuously. As long as the source—the pumps—were energized, the fountain was actuated.

If God is the pump—the source of energy that produces the fountain of joy in our lives—then our fountain of joy will continue to flow until His energy is exhausted. Can you think of anything that would interrupt the energy of the life of God? Through all eternity, God—the source of our joy and energy that excites that joy into a glorious display of beauty and melody—will remain constant.

The Joy That Fills Heaven

The fifth reason I call our joy eternal is because heaven is filled with gloriously expressed joy. Reread the book of Revelation and see what the saints who have already entered that glorious realm are doing. You'll see them expressing their joy in every way we have mentioned in this book. They sing, dance, shout, bow, kneel, march, wave palm fronds, and behave like children at a Sunday school picnic. There are many scenes of uninhibited joy and all of them are accepted by the One who sits on the throne.

What a delight this will be! We are limited in our earthly expressions of joy by our physical condition. Reginald Heber reminds us, "Eternity has no gray hairs! The flowers fade, the heart withers, man grows old and dies, the world lies down in the sepulcher of ages, but time writes no wrinkles on the brow of eternity."[8] The joys with which we enter heaven will never fade; they will only increase in beauty, magnitude, and expression.

Yes! Joy is a blessed gift, an active power. Where it is imparted to a believer's life, it will induce a rejoicing that expresses that joy, but all of this is only a rehearsal. The real concert of joy will be in heaven where we'll join multitudes of the redeemed crying, *"Hosanna; Blessed is he that cometh in the name of the Lord"* (Mark 11:9*b*), and join the angels in saying, *"Glory to God in the highest..."* (Luke 2:14).

Joy is eternal and we now have eternal life. Let your joy splash out on all those who have not received their touch of eternity. It may make them jealous enough to turn to God.

For Reflection

1. If gladness is impermanent and happiness is transient, where do we place joy?
2. To think of eternity as being unchanging and everlasting doesn't fit our current frame of reference. Can you think of an example that illustrates eternity?
3. Give three of the five reasons I listed for considering our joy eternal.
4. Share your testimony regarding the precious gift of joy. In the telling, you will find the fountain of joy soaring ever higher in your life.

Endnotes
1. Maurice Maeterlinck (1862-1949), Entry 3267, *Draper's Book of Quotations for the Christian World*, Edythe Draper, Copyright © 1992 by Tyndale House Publishers, Inc., Wheaton, IL.
2. Ibid., Elias Canetti (1905-), Entry 3276.

3. Ibid., Hendrick Willem Van Loon (1882-1944), Entry 3273.

4. Fanny J. Crosby, "Blessed Assurance." Public domain.

5. C.S. Lewis—James S. Hewett, *Illustrations Unlimited*, page 172, Copyright © 1988 by Tyndale House Publishers, Inc., Wheaton, IL.

6. Sir Thomas Browne (1605-1682), Entry 3284, *Draper's Book of Quotations for the Christian World*, Edythe Draper, Copyright © 1992 by Tyndale House Publishers, Inc., Wheaton, IL.

7. Ibid., A.W. Tozer (1897-1963), Entry 3274.

8. Ibid., Reginald Heber (1783-1826), Entry 3266.

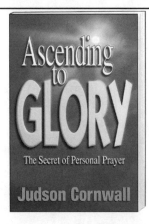

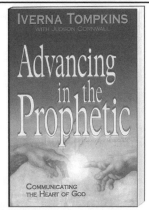

Finally, there is one source for all your *renewal resources!*

Whether you are looking for the latest books from Iverna Tompkins, Rick Joyner or Fuchsia Pickett, or a timeless spiritual masterpiece by Smith Wigglesworth, *WindsofFire.com* has them all. *WindsofFire.com* is your one stop store for all your renewal and revival resources.

Here's what you'll discover at WindsofFire.com:

- The most banned and burned book in Christian history
- God showed this leading Bible scholar a vision of the coming revival. Be prepared.
- The greatest Christian writer since the apostle Paul — learn about the book that sent her to prison.

- The hottest and best-selling books on the cutting edge of what God is doing on the earth today
- Life-changing messages on cassette

So visit **WindsofFire.com** today and find all your renewal resources